SCIENCE AND TECHNOLOGY
FOR DEVELOPMENT

About the series

Development Matters is a series of comprehensive but concise introductions to the key issues in development studies. It offers politically engaged and challenging critiques while demonstrating academic and conceptual rigour to provide readers with critical, reflexive and challenging explorations of the pressing concerns in development. With carefully designed features, such as explanatory text boxes, glossaries and recommended reading, the series provides the reader with accessible guides to development studies.

Series editors: Helen Yanacopulos and Matt Bailie Smith

About the author

James Smith is co-director of the Centre of African Studies at the University of Edinburgh. He is also a director of the ESRC Innogen Research Centre at Edinburgh and a visiting fellow in development policy and practice at The Open University. His research explores the relationships between knowledge, science and development, particularly in relation to agricultural research and how it is practised. He has worked with many international organizations and research centres, including Oxfam, DFID, IDRC and the Consultative Group for International Agricultural Research.

SCIENCE AND TECHNOLOGY
FOR DEVELOPMENT

DEVELOPMENT **MATTERS**

JAMES SMITH

Zed Books
London & New York

Science and Technology for Development was first published in 2009 by Zed Books Ltd, 7 Cynthia Street, London N1 9JF, UK and Room 400, 175 Fifth Avenue, New York, NY 10010, USA

www.zedbooks.co.uk

Typeset in the UK by Long House Publishing Services
Index by Mike Kirkwood
Cover designed by Rogue Four Design

A catalogue record for this book is available from the British Library
Library of Congress Cataloging in Publication Data available

ISBN 978 1 84813 200 9 hb
ISBN 978 1 84813 201 6 pb
ISBN 978 1 84813 202 3 eb

Contents

Acknowledgements

This book is partially based on primary research undertaken over the past four years and I would like to thank the various organizations that have made this work possible. The UK Economic and Social Research Council, through the Innogen Centre, provided many of the resources to undertake fieldwork in Africa, Asia and Latin America. Smaller elements of the research were funded by the MacArthur Foundation, the Microsoft Foundation and the UK Department for International Development. The University of Edinburgh gave me time off from teaching and administration to undertake research and write sections of the book. Several organizations assisted me in various other ways: the African Centre of Technology Studies, the International Livestock Research Institute, the International Rice Research Institute, the Centro Internacional de la Papa, the International Aids Vaccine Initiative and the Food and Agriculture Organization of the United Nations. I would like to thank the series editors, Helen Yanacopulos and Matt Smith, and the Zed Books editor, Tamsine O'Riordan, for their helpful comments on an earlier draft. Several colleagues have helped in innumerable ways, not least Peter Bryant, Joanna Chataway, Norman Clark, Lawrence Dritsas, Andy Hall, Becky Hanlin, Matt Harsh, Maija Hirvonen, Ian Maudlin, Tom Molony, Olga Morawczynski, Julius Mugwagwa, Lois Muraguri, Joyce Tait and David Wield. Last and not least I would like to thank my impossibly patient partner, Barbara, who had to deal with my writing in the midst of her own writing projects. Deadlines have a habit of attracting each other.

Acronyms

CGIAR	Consultative Group on International Agricultural Research
CIMMYT	Centro Internacional de Mejoramiento de Maíz y Trigo (International Maize and Wheat Improvement Centre)
DDT	dichloro-diphenyl-trichloroethane
DFID	Department for International Development
FAO	Food and Agriculture Organization of the United Nations
GM/GMO	genetically modified/genetically modified organism
GNP	Gross National Product
HIV	Human Immunodeficiency Virus
HYV	high-yielding variety
IARCs	International Agricultural Research Centres
ICRISAT	International Crops Research Institute for the Semi-Arid Tropics
ICTs	information and communication technologies
IDEs	International Development Enterprises
ILCA	International Livestock Centre for Africa
ILRAD	International Laboratory for Research on Animal Diseases
ILRI	International Livestock Research Institute
IPR	intellectual property rights
IRRI	International Rice Research Institute
MDGs	Millennium Development Goals

MEP	Malaria Eradication Programme
MSF	Médecins Sans Frontières
NARS	National Agricultural Research Systems
NGO	non-governmental organization
TRIPS	trade-related aspects of intellectual property rights
USAID	United States Agency for International Development
WHO	World Health Organization

Foreword

This is one of those rare books that brings out the complex web of relationships among science, technology and development with great clarity and originality. The author, Dr James Smith, has analysed several models of institution building and has highlighted the need for an approach which will lead to social inclusion in access to technologies. Science is obviously the means to expanding the frontiers of knowledge, while technology helps to convert scientific knowledge into processes and products which can confer benefits relevant to human needs. It has become increasingly clear, particularly after the realization that for development to be sustainable over time, there is need to consider not only economic and environmental issues, but also the social dimension. This is where new thinking and proactive analysis of the consequences of the spread of modern technologies become important. In January 1968 (before the term 'Green Revolution' was coined), while addressing the Indian Science Congress, I emphasized the need for a proactive action–reaction analysis in relation to technology development and dissemination.

> Exploitive agriculture offers great dangers if carried out with only an immediate profit or production motive. The emerging exploitive farming community in India should become aware of this. Intensive cultivation of land without conservation of soil fertility and soil structure would lead, ultimately, to the springing up of deserts. Irrigation without arrangements for drainage would result in soils getting alkaline or saline. Indiscriminate use of

pesticides, fungicides and herbicides could cause adverse changes in biological balance as well as lead to an increase in the incidence of cancer and other diseases, through the toxic residues present in the grains or other edible parts. Unscientific tapping of underground water will lead to the rapid exhaustion of this wonderful capital resource left to us through ages of natural farming. The rapid replacement of numerous locally adapted varieties with one or two high-yielding strains in large contiguous areas would result in the spread of serious diseases capable of wiping out entire crops, as happened prior to the Irish potato famine of 1854 and the Bengal rice famine in 1942. Therefore the initiation of exploitive agriculture without a proper understanding of the various consequences of every one of the changes introduced into traditional agriculture, and without first building up a proper scientific and training base to sustain it, may only lead us, in the long run, into an era of agricultural disaster rather than one of agricultural prosperity.

Taking the examples of the International Rice Research Institute in the Philippines and the International Livestock Research Institute in Nairobi, Dr Smith has provided a framework for shifting from Mode 1 Knowledge, which is more academic, discipline-based and initiated by the researcher, to Mode 2 Knowledge, which involves constantly changing multi-disciplinary teams working on specific problems relevant to the real world. It is obvious that in cases of original and strategic research, there is need for a Mode 1 approach. Where the aim, as for example in agriculture, is the enhancement of productivity and profitability of major crops there is need to take into account the wide variability prevailing in growing and socio-economic conditions. This will be obvious from the fact that over 125,000 strains of rice exist in the gene banks of IRRI and other national genetic resource conservation centres.

The world is witnessing an increasing number of divides. The latest in the series is a digital divide. A gender divide in relation to access to technologies is widespread and is one of the causes for gender inequity. The mobile phone is an example of a technology which can help to reach the unreached and voice the voiceless. The challenge for development leaders is in harnessing relevant and environmentally benign technologies as allies in the movement for social, economic and gender equity. This will also call for a mindset change among science planners and research leaders. For example, advances in medical sciences have helped to add years to life. However, only specific human goals and spiritual values can add life to years. This is where the initiative of the small kingdom of Bhutan in replacing the concept of Gross National Product (GNP) with Gross National Happiness (GNH) is an important one. Happiness is more than mere economic growth or technological advance.

We owe a deep debt of gratitude to Dr James Smith for bringing together, in this very readable book, a large amount of critical and analytical thinking and experience that show how science, technology and development can become mutually reinforcing. The book is particularly a must-read for schools designed to breed a new class of researchers, planners, strategists and implementers. Only then will we enter an era of humanistic science and scientific humanism.

Professor M. S. Swaminathan
Founder and Chairman, M. S. Swaminathan Foundation

Introduction | Development and the Promise of Technology

Technology is inextricably linked to development. Neither exists without the other, each propels the other along, and the successes and failures of both are bound together. However we choose to conceive of development, as a deeply historical process of change or as the small-scale activities non-governmental organizations (NGOs) engage in, as macro-economic policy or as community development, technology is always present. Technology is most visible in the headline-grabbing impacts of the Green Revolution, the search for a vaccine for HIV, or, more recently, in debates around the positive or negative impacts of biofuel production. Technology, though, is not only about vaccines, biotechnologies or climate change; it concerns almost everything we do, or hope to do. We are embedded in technology, we consume technology and it subsumes our identities, shapes how we interact with the world, and circumscribes our future, whether in terms of risks or benefits. Mobile phones can connect the disconnected and lonely, transportation allows us to visit new places, and improvements in agriculture have, for some at least, left us less hungry or even overweight. Society and technology are mutually constitutive.

Technology has had many far-reaching impacts on development. The 'Green Revolution' – the international effort to increase agricultural production of staple crops such as rice and wheat through the development and dissemination of new seed varieties in the 1960s and 1970s – saw massive increases in yields of staple crops across large swathes of South Asia (Evanson and

Gollin, 2003).[1] Management of disease-transmitting insects (termed 'vectors') such as tsetse fly and mosquitoes reduced the impacts of insect-borne disease in many contexts. Mass vaccination programmes reduced the impact of diseases such as polio in developing countries. Access to new forms of energy – hydro-electricity, solar energy, bio-based sources – ensures households have light and a means to cook. Each of these examples has a caveat, however. For example, the Green Revolution was generally unable to significantly increase yields in more marginal areas, and demanded that farmers engage in new and more intensive forms of agricultural production, in some cases dramatically altering their livelihoods and the risks they were obliged to take (Lipton and Longhurst, 1989). Many insect vectors have developed resistance to chemical pesticides and these pesticides, too, have their own environmental implications (Carson, 2002). The fact that an oral polio-immunization campaign was set up by outsiders and not as a part of normal healthcare infrastructure led to distrust and fed into existing political tension in Muslim northern Nigeria (Leach, 2007). Hydro-electricity schemes have led to massive forced removals of communities and loss of biodiversity (Scudder, 2005) and emerging technologies for energy provision such as biofuels are becoming increasingly mired in debate around efficiency, impact and implications for food security and soaring food prices (Wetlands International, 2006).

These examples represent neither miracles, technological panaceas, nor unfettered disasters. Rather, they represent the enormous complexities of the interrelationships between science, technology and society. Unforeseen outcomes, hidden relationships, shifting contexts or unproven technologies all agglomerate to change trajectories of knowledge accumulation or refract the implications of technologies and their impact on society. Science is increasingly contested, much as development is, but more often than not its implications, how it will interact with society and what its impacts will be, can only be understood fully in retro-spect. This unknowing, or inability to foresee all outcomes with regard to science and technology, has led to many of the contes-tations and controversies regarding new technologies we have witnessed.

Meanwhile the call for science and technology for develop-ment is getting louder and the pace of change accelerating. The 2002 World Summit on Sustainable Development underlined the importance of science and technology for global development. The 2005 Report of the Commission for Africa (*Our Common Interest*) recommended that US$3 billion should be invested in developing centres of excellence in science and technology. Global science-led initiatives such as the International Aids Vaccine Initiative (IAVI), the Global Fund to Fight AIDS, Tuberculosis and Malaria and the Consultative Group on International Agricultural Research (CGIAR) attract hundreds of millions of pounds of funding. Bilateral and multilateral donors are increasingly recognizing the importance of science and tech-nology for development by investing more resources in science and technology research and global science initiatives such as those listed above (World Bank, 1999; UNDP, 2001). According to the 2005 UN Millennium Project on Science, Technology and Innovation, all eight Millennium Development Goals (MDGs)[2] depend to greater or lesser extents on adequate investment in science and technology (Juma and Yee-Cheong, 2005). Allied to the clamour for increased emphasis and investment, indeed in some respects driving the clamour, is the lure of new generic tech-nologies, so-called 'platform technologies',[3] such as information and communication technologies (ICTs), biotechnologies and nanotechnologies, which promise much in many areas of our lives, in some respects to transform our lives. Meanwhile, in terms such as the 'digital divide' or the 'molecular divide' we can discern some of the core problems with technology for development. How can we make sure that the poorest and most vulnerable communities have access to appropriate technologies? Who decides what technologies the poorest communities most need? And who decides what science is funded to bring these technologies into existence?[4] The relationship between science, technology and development has been described as a 'fast race' (Leach and Scoones, 2006): a race to use science and technology to spur economic growth, and a race to find technological fixes to solve developmental problems. The promise of new technologies to act as transformational economic and developmental agents is thought to be worth investing in, or gambling on, and on occasion that promise may blind us to the risks.

Science and technology have played a central historical role in development efforts, but not an unproblematic one. Increasingly, science and technology are being touted as the core or driver of future development efforts, and are shaping how development is organized, how it is conceptualized and how it is practised. Development itself is a highly contested term and possesses multiple meanings in different contexts. Development is notoriously difficult to define, science and technology only slightly less so, but however equivocally we choose to articulate 'development' and 'science' and 'technology', a complex set of mutually supportive articulations remains. It has become almost *passé* to quote Harry Truman's Inaugural Address when talking about development, but it is not being used here to mark the beginning of any grand process of 'development' but instead to underline how historically entrenched science, technology and development are:

> We must embark on a bold new program for making the benefits of our scientific advances and industrial progress available for the improvement and growth of underdeveloped areas. More than half the people of the world are living in conditions approaching misery. Their food is inadequate. They are victims of disease. Their economic life is primitive and stagnant. Their poverty is a

handicap and threat both to them and to more prosperous areas. For the first time in history, humanity possesses the knowledge and skill to relieve the suffering of these people. . . . I believe that we should make available to peace-loving peoples the benefits of our store of technical knowledge in order to help them realize their aspirations for a better life. (Public Papers of the Presidents of the United States, 1964: 114–15)

In Truman's narrative, science and technology are sutured together with economic development to drive a process that will lift people out of poverty, heal their illnesses, fill their bellies and draw a veil of aspiration, prosperity and peace over the world. Escobar (1995) and others have used Truman's quote to notate a moment when development, or perhaps more accurately under-development, was first proclaimed as a global concern. There is a risk in focusing on moments that periodize development or over-stating speeches as indicative of any meta-narrative of develop-ment, but Truman's speech certainly spoke to a genuine optimism that technology and economic development, carefully nurtured and guided by the West, could lead to development on the grandest scale. This sense of optimism can be traced through many of the large-scale technological initiatives that have punctu-ated development, some of which are discussed in this book.

Truman's narrative also portrays a particular perspective of science and technology, similar to what can be described as a fifty-year-old 'pre-history' to science and technology studies: the study of understanding, explaining and ultimately reinforcing science, without questioning its basis. In this 'pre-history' we can sketch out a common view of science as a formal activity that accumulates knowledge by directly confronting the natural world. Science progresses because of its method, and that method allows the natural world to act as a sort of laboratory for the evaluation of theories. Science's method is a set of tools and approaches that makes research systematic and replicable, and tends towards the discovery of truths. While the scientific method may be varied and complex and may not smooth all inaccuracies, it does nevertheless allow a level of consistency: different scientists should be able to replicate experiments; scientists should be able to agree on important questions and theories; and, most importantly, different scientists should accept or reject the same hypotheses when presented with the same data. The result is that only scientists can arrive at 'truths' about the natural world. One by-product of this view of how science works was that scientists were afforded an essentialist, privileged position in society as they were seen to give impartial, rational advice (Sismondo, 2004). They were able to speak truths. There are telling parallels not only between this account of science and Truman's account of how scientific advances would solve developmental problems, but also between science and development itself. Development would confront its own natural world, and accumulate knowledge in confrontation with it. Development was thought to be systematic and replicable; this would ease the transposition of ideas and approaches from the developed to the undeveloped world. Development possessed its own way of viewing the world, and its own 'method' that would create 'truths' regarding the world's problems. Ultimately, development also became a 'truth', essentialized and universalized as something that 'humanity' must undertake.

Typically, the development of technology has been understood through a familiar linear pattern. Technology was long thought of as the straightforward application of science. Technologists would identify needs, problems or opportunities and craft pieces of scientific knowledge into technological artefacts to deal with them (Sismondo, 2004). This linearity echoes the 'linear progressions and optimistic teleologies' of an expected march to a more modern, progressive world in Africa and elsewhere (Ferguson, 1999: 13). The fact that we need the eight Millennium

Development Goals to galvanize efforts demonstrates optimism has been largely misplaced and progression less than straightforward. This, then, is the starting point for this book. The aim is not to provide a systematic overview of technologies *for* development. It is not a manual of developmental artefacts and their application. Rather it is an attempt to draw on critical thinking in development studies and science and technology studies to help us better understand the complex relationship between science, technology and development.

Science and technology studies

Science and technology have been referred to as the 'dark matter' of the social sciences (Latour, 1992). Despite our lives being so firmly meshed with science and technology that it is impossible to conceive of where we end and technology begins, let alone try to imagine life without technology, social studies of technology have been relatively sparse, until recently at least. This 'dark matter' holds society together, precisely because it allows us to live our lives, relate to others and perhaps even fulfil a 'totality of being' in the modern world. Machines and the other products of science and technology are societal glue as well as material objects. People and institutions continue to dominate the social sciences, however. Science and technology studies makes a social-constructivist case for understanding science, scientific interpretations of the world and technologies as actors in the world (cf. Knorr-Cetina, 1981 or Barnes *et al.*, 1996). Science and technology studies reconceptualized science as a social and political activity and this cast science's framing of questions, its development of methodologies, its modes of investigation and analysis, its means of reaching consensus, and its dealings with risk and uncertainty in whole new lights (Leach *et al.*, 2005).

Science and technology studies ultimately stem from an understanding that science and technology are fundamentally social activities. The long-held view of science is devoid of people (or at least their influence), much in the same way that fifty-year-old narratives of development were devoid of communities and societies other than populations to be labelled as 'backward' or 'primitive', on the one hand, or 'developed' on the other (Escobar, 1995). For science and technology studies there is no abstract scientific method. Scientists, engineers and technologists are members of communities and all that entails: rules, norms, and institutions. They are trained to be members of epistemic communities and are measured against the rules of those communities; they adhere to prevailing methods of enquiry; try to conform to indicators of excellence; and communicate using rhetorical devices born out of their communities. Communication is central to this as actors in science and technology are continually obliged to sell their positions to peers and others. They are engaged in a constant struggle for resources, opportunities and outlets for their ideas. In contraposition to any traditional, rational conception of science, ideology, values and other mechanisms of persuasion are deeply embedded within all scientific practice (Sismondo, 2004). Science and technology studies reject the essentialist view that scientific knowledge is somehow more 'pure', exemplary or 'truthful' than other types of knowledge, or that scientists and technologists undertake their work inoculated from the politics of their own communities of practice or from the macroscopic spheres of politics and ideology. By maintaining a symmetry of explanation, of treating all kinds of knowledge equally and adopting an impartial approach to explaining people's beliefs, whether they be 'scientific' or 'non-scientific', science and technology studies has attempted to place science firmly in a social and cultural context (Bloor, 1991).

Studying science, technology and development

Even in this very short introduction it is clear there are reso-
nances and contiguities between science and technology studies
and 'critical' development studies (with its concern with
adopting social-constructivist, anti-essentialist positions regarding development knowledge and the power and practices of
development). This is intuitive given that science and development operate in similar and related ways: each seeks to define
itself as an exemplary form of knowledge based on either
scientific method or on some sort of moral authority and
inevitability (or more tellingly a combination of both). Each
revolves around an historically teleological vision of progress,
innovation and a future. Each makes use of complex rhetorical
devices and communities of practice to construct its own 'black
boxes'.[5] These similarities are compounded, of course, and
indeed strengthened, by the close interrelationship between
development and technology.

Both critical development studies and science and technology
studies seek to place the social at the heart of their analyses.
Development, even (if not especially) the rhetorical 'development'
of Truman and the Millennium Development Goals, is a social
activity in much the same way science is. Both disciplines recognize that neither development nor science is an exemplary, essentialist form of knowledge. Both are critical of purely linear narratives – for which there is only one trajectory of development or
one way in which a new technology will diffuse, implying that
history, rather than reflecting the outcomes of struggles within
society, becomes a vacuum in which cultural and political
processes play no meaningful role. In fact, understanding historical context often lies at the core of their analyses.

Science and technology studies and critical development
studies (or post-development studies)[6] take anti-essentialist

positions with respect to science and technology and development. Neither science, technology nor development demonstrate simple properties that define them once and for all. The sources of all knowledge and the artefacts or processes that derive from them are complex and context-bound. There is no scientific method to translate nature into knowledge, and no technological method to translate knowledge into artefacts, much as there is no singular developmental approach to reduce inequality by identifying it, or promote growth by forecasting it. Critical perspectives on science, technology and development must investigate how knowledge and its products are constructed as the outcomes of social interaction, within context.

Neither critical development studies nor science and technology studies seek to reject either development or technology. Rather, both fields of study seek to place due emphasis on their subject precisely by taking care to develop understandings of context, process and critique. Mainstream development has led to enormous improvements in many people's lives, and can continue to do so. Similarly, science and technology have wrought social transformations that we could not have dreamt of only a few decades ago. Neither is perfect, and perhaps neither claims to be, but both are fundamental in shaping the social and material worlds in which we live, particularly in developing countries. Development, in using science and technology, seeks to improve our lives and fulfil our wants and needs, or at least stimulate those wants and needs, and for that reason it is important that we take due care in understanding how technology for development has impacted upon our world and how it will continue to do so in the future.

Further reading

Harding, S. (2008) *Sciences From Below: Feminisms, Postcolonialisms and Modernities,* Duke University Press, Durham NC.

Mackenzie, D. and J. Wacjman (1999) *The Social Shaping of Technology,* Open University Press, London.

Sismondo, S. (2004) *An Introduction to Science and Technology Studies,* Blackwell, Oxford.

Yearley, S. (2005) *Making Sense of Science: Understanding the Social Study of Science,* Sage, London.

1 | Rethinking Technology for Development

The role of technology as an engine (or perhaps more accurately the driver) of development has been a constant since colonial times. There are striking parallels between science and colonialism and technology and modern development – a coupling of science and technology and economic development to forge change, to generate new connections within the world and transform societies into facsimiles of an idealized social order in the name of 'progress' (Ferguson, 2004). Within these ideas is a strong sense of the certainty and inevitability of change, a feeling that the future can be mapped out, and implicit within this is the notion that past histories and context are somehow unimportant. Only the future counts.

More explicitly in the case of modern development, theory holds that technology and economic development can generate new connections within the world, and transform 'developing countries' into their modern, industrialized, developed counterparts; this would advance humanity 'from kinship to contract, agriculture to industry, personalized to rational or bureaucratic rule, subsistence to capital accumulation and mass consumption, tradition to modernity and poverty to wealth' (Edelman and Haugerud, 2005: 2). The idea of a linear trajectory from one stage to another, from pre-technological to technological, from traditional to modern, from indigenous to scientific is implicit within most mainstream development thinking, and was implicit – if perhaps considered less of a priority – in most colonial thinking. Colonial and development thinking, so different in terms of aim and ideology, are stitched together by the shared idea of the application of technology.

The introductory chapter quoted Harry Truman's inaugural address as an illustration of how closely the relationship between technology and development was conceived: global poverty would be solved by vigorous application of modern scientific and technical knowledge (Truman, [1949] 1964). Development remains as bound up and enamoured with science and technology as colonialism was, and certainly as Harry Truman was. Indeed, if anything, a series of recent high-profile initiatives, reports and policy documents have signalled a renewed belief (and calls for renewed investment) in the role science and technology should play in development. For example, the United Nations Millennium Project Task Force on Science, Technology and Innovation reiterates the need to harness science and technology sustainably to accelerate development (Juma and Yee-Cheong, 2005). The October 2004 UK House of Commons Science and Technology Committee report on 'The Use of Science in UK International Development Policy' drew on a wide range of expert knowledge to illustrate the importance of generating real capacity through development, partnerships, and science and technological innovation. Building science and technological capacity is seen as a lever to draw together the 'yawning divide between North and South' (House of Commons, 2004: 44). The Commission for Africa report, *Our Common Interest,* juxtaposes our ability to map the human genome and 'clone a human being' with our inability to prevent African women from dying in childbirth. Africa's lack of investment in science and technology is contrasted to Asia's investment. The document calls for a series of centres of science and technology excellence to be set up across the continent (Commission for Africa, 2005).

This chapter seeks to examine why science and technology are regarded so universally as the lever through which development can be ratcheted up a notch or two, and in doing so will discuss ways in which we can undertake a more critical exploration of the relationship between science, technology and development. Case studies of trajectories of development in various countries, seed breeding in Southern Africa, information and communication technologies, and science policy, amongst others, are used to illustrate some of the thinking and narratives that have driven science and technology as the key to development.

Modernization, linear progressions and 'technological determinism'

Rostow, in his highly influential *Non-Communist Manifesto* (1960), elaborated a 'take-off' that all countries would eventually achieve (note the technological metaphor). Rostow characterized countries as passing from one stage to another of a five-stage model; from 'traditional society' characterized by 'pre-Newtonian' technology and little rational decision making, through a pre-take-off stage, then 'take-off' in which 'traditional' impediments to economic growth are overcome, to a 'drive to maturity' which is marked by technological innovation and enlargement of the industrial base, and finally to the 'age of mass consumption', exhibiting widespread affluence, urbanization and the consumption of 'consumer durables'. In all these stages Rostow was careful to couple advancing technology and new knowledge (in giving up 'traditional' ideas) to economic development and industrial modernization.

Development in this context becomes a macro-economic drive towards modernity, 'an expression of modernity on a planetary scale' (Berthoud, 1991: 23). Rostow sought to develop a rejection of the inevitabilities that Marx portrayed in *Capital* but in the process succeeded in producing something similar in the narrative of the 'inevitability of take-off' it portrayed. In some respects it projected something even grander, an inevitable transformation of every country, if they were to follow the rules. From a different perspective this can be seen in terms of a discourse of the 'non-existent': developing countries may desire to become developed, but cannot because something is missing (Sorj, 1991). Rostow's ideas, and the concept of modernization they influenced, represent a highly temporalized historical sequence: poor people and poor countries 'were not simply at the bottom, they were at the beginning' (Ferguson, 2006: 178). From this perspective, development would be the 'black box' that would enable take-off, while the poor, the 'less developed', were expected to be passive receivers of development, of Western values, knowledge and technology (Rist, 1997).

The UN Millennium Report on Science and Technology for Development echoes Rostowian and modernization theory: 'Economic historians suggest that the prime explanation for the success of today's advanced industrial countries lies in their history of innovation along different dimensions: institutions, technology, trade, organization, and the application of natural resources' (Juma and Yee-Cheong, 2005: 27). The report goes on to discuss the economic development of Finland, asserting that since the 1980s it has transformed itself from a country dependent on natural resources to one at the top of the list of most indices of global competitiveness by investing heavily in research and development and reformulating its support for education, research and innovation (*ibid.*: 28). Finland – economically, developmentally, geographically, and perhaps in any way one can think of – is clearly very different from the average developing country. Nevertheless, it is offered as a blueprint. The report cites a World Bank-funded study that developed four categories of countries:

scientifically advanced, scientifically proficient, scientifically developing, and scientifically lagging countries (Wagner *et al.*, 2001). In this formulation, the role of technology is foregrounded as the determining factor that drives development. Where development has not occurred or has been slow, the limiting factor has been a lack of technology, a lack of access to technology, or a lack of the knowledge necessary to use technology. To invest in the promise of technology is to profit in progress. Not investing in technology means lacking a fundament of progress, development and modernization.

Asian Tigers and the role of technology

The idea of 'technological catch-up' is frequently referred to as a means by which poorer, 'follower' countries can catch up with and even, in some respects, overtake richer, 'leader' countries (Forbes and Wield, 2002). Much of this work is derived from a different economic tradition than the neoclassical economics of Rostow and modernization theorists (for example, Juma and Clark, 2002). Evolutionary economics argues that rather than converging towards the economies and levels of productivity of the more developed countries, countries may follow different paths. There are various factors that can allow countries to jump-start their economies, including the ability of governments to design and implement appropriate economic policies and the technological and skill level of the population. Many of these policies and the need to develop a country's skill base are highlighted in research (Abramovitz, 1989; Makinda, 2007) and reports such as the *UN Millennium Report* (Juma and Yee-Cheong, 2005). New technologies, too, may offer the opportunity for countries to develop niches for themselves (Meier, 2000; Niosi and Reid, 2007). One important caveat is that it is generally the larger, more advanced economies that have the potential to harness and profit from new technologies such as biotechnology, nanotechnology or information and communication technologies. In many cases the Rostowian problematic of just how does one evolve from one stage to the next remains unsolved, and the narrative of progress remains central to alternative models of economic development.

'Technological catch-up' remains an idea that many countries aspire to, a condition that much policy is developed to support, and an enterprise many institutions are set up to develop. Unfortunately, it seems the capacity and resources needed to harness technology as a driver of economic growth are in themselves manifestations of economic growth. Progression seems intuitive in theory, but much more complex in practice; effectively harnessing technology to aid economic growth remains the capacity of well-developed, modern economies and these disparities have not proved easy to short-circuit. Evolutionary economics presents an alternative perspective on economic development to Rostow, but in tying technology and economic growth tightly together it presents another take on modernization theory. Huge disparities in wealth, resources and capacity to innovate and utilize technologies mean that 'catch-up' is difficult to achieve on a broad scale and we risk falling back into simple narratives of technological determinism.

However, the four East Asian 'Tiger' economies are frequently cited as examples that offer hope to developing countries and a model they should aspire to in terms of economic development, modernization and 'catch-up'.[7] Until the stock market crash of the late 1990s, the Asian Pacific was considered to be the world's success story of economic development and technological modernization. Hong Kong, South Korea, Singapore and Taiwan enjoyed average annual growth rates of GNP of between 8.9 per cent and 7.5 per cent between 1965 and 1996 (during which time

Different stripes: the four Asian Tigers

Superficially, the four Asian Tigers state a good case for modernization theory: each economy was able, to varying degrees, to adapt to the changing pattern of the global economy through technological upgrading, market expansion and economic diversification, and in doing this relied on an educated, highly productive and flexible labour force. In addition, all these countries developed a focus on the exportation of manufactured goods, whilst to varying degrees protecting their own economies through state control and economic barriers. Yet they achieved their undoubted success in quite different ways. Singapore's industrialization was centred on the state's relationship to multinational companies; in South Korea industry was heavily controlled and nurtured by the state; while Taiwan blended small and medium family business networks with a few large, national firms. Hong Kong's economic growth, by contrast, was engineered through small, local manufacturing firms, supported by a state that provided protective infrastructure and subsidized collective consumption. Each country focused on expanding and then diversifying different sectors of its economy. The city states of Hong Kong and Singapore provided a welfare state of sorts. This was not the case in South Korea, where some workers' needs were catered for by industry, or in Taiwan, where education was provided by the state, but the trickle-down effects of economic growth were left to cater for other needs (Castells, 1998). It is clear, as Castells states, that:

> [E]ach case was dependent upon the specific set of relationships between the state, economy and society. Thus, we need to explain, at the same time, why each economy developed. . . . It is in the interplay of internal social dynamics and external financial flows, both mediated by the institutions of the state, that the explanation for the contradictory process of Asian Pacific development and crisis lies. (*Ibid.*: 219)

the growth rate for the world at large was 3.1 per cent) (Castells, 1998). Manuel Castells has provided a detailed comparative analysis of the causes and trajectories of development of the four countries, and what is most striking are the differences.

The cases of the four Asian Tiger economies are useful in two ways. First, they stress the role technological development can play in economic growth and development: their success was based on investing in technology integrated into their economies. By contrast, many Latin American countries invested in science and research, for example in building excellent universities, but this did not translate into economic gains on the scale the Asian Pacific enjoyed.[8] Second, they underline that societies are not global and uniform, but profoundly historically and culturally rooted. Simple narratives of modernization are often guilty of not appreciating this diversity. What worked for European countries is not what worked for the Asian Tigers – and neither is it likely to be what will work in Africa and South Asia. Within these histories it is important to recognize that the role of technology is contingent and not unitary.

Claims for technology and the knowledge to create it also risk a-historicizing development. There is almost a sense that all developing countries lack is science, knowledge and technology: 'the entire international system of stratification has come to be based not on "who owns what" but on "who knows what"' (Mazrui and White, 1988: 359), or 'Africa's poverty and lack of global influence appear to stem from its weak technological and knowledge base' (Makinda, 2007: 973). No serious historian of African or Third World underdevelopment would attribute global inequalities solely to 'who knows what'. Wiping away the context in which technology can play an important role in development is not likely to ensure its effectiveness or help us understand what roles science and technology can play. Indeed, it almost serves to divorce science and technology from society and the economy, which, as we can see with the Asian Tigers, is where it is effective. Ultimately, in focusing almost solely on knowledge we risk ignoring the enormous structural and infrastructural constraints developing countries face.

Technological determinism and societal change

These calls for investment in more and better knowledge in science and technology are not simply calls for new technologies to be transferred from North to South, or from laboratory to field. They are calls for the creation of new technological spaces: new ways of thinking about science and technology, new places where technologies can be created, new policies to support science for development, and new societal configurations which can assimilate, adapt and absorb new technologies. The *UN Millennium Report* talks not of 'simply . . . installing devices, but [of] transforming society and its value systems' (Juma and Yee-Cheong, 2005: 15). It is clearly not sufficient to think of technology antiseptically as something inert, neutral and devoid of its own context, as something that will exist through knowledge, as something to be transferred via a sort of developmental osmotic potential or summoned through the calculus of poverty. Somewhat paradoxically, the problem is identified as a simple deficiency in knowledge; the solution is presented as an entire reworking of society and its value systems in order to harness technology. Modernization theory proposes a sort of technological determinism in which the technology is obscured or absent (Smith and Marx, 1994).[9] Developing countries need technology, but as they lack the knowledge to use technology productively they need to reorganize to develop the skills and knowledge to do so. Policy, in proposing something simple, is in fact promoting something profound and transformational. Technology, or in the case of developing countries its relative absence, prescribes a certain type of society in order to drive progress. While it is indeed true that to harness technology effectively for economic growth countries need to establish the conditions and expertise to do so, as the Asian Tigers did in their different ways, we need to think very carefully about the implications of reconfiguring society for technology and the effects of technology on society. It is wholly insufficient to talk only in terms of 'deficits', 'investment' and 'transformation'; the impact of technology is far more profound than that.

The reflexivity of the Green Revolution

The Green Revolution has been used to describe the systematic and centralized development of new hybrid cereal varieties and agricultural management practices that were introduced across Asia in the 1960s and 1970s. The ethos of the Green Revolution developed with the transformation of agriculture that began in Mexico with the development of high-yielding hybrid varieties of wheat and in the Philippines with the development of hybrid varieties of rice. Modern, Western scientific approaches to crop breeding were applied to the problem of low and declining crop yields and this highly focused approach resulted in the release of a succession of new varieties of staple crops such as rice and wheat with the potential to provide much higher yields under optimum conditions. It was assumed that applying scientific techniques that had worked in North America and Europe would produce similar agricultural development in less developed countries. The focus was very much on producing new varieties of crops; little initial attention was focused on how agriculture was practised, how farmers would adopt new varieties and what the consequences of these new crop varieties would be. There was an associated transformation in agriculture related to how agricultural research was undertaken, agricultural extension, the use of inputs like fertilizers, and the introduction of technologies such as irrigation systems (some of these issues are discussed in more detail in the next chapter). The Green Revolution raised average cereal yields but the impacts were not uniform and some suggest long-term social and ecological problems were provoked.

These innovations had very positive effects on aggregate yields, but very varied impacts in differing contexts. Many critiques of the Green Revolution point to the way hybrid crop varieties, with their demands for fertilizers, irrigation, the purchase of seeds and the like forced small-scale farmers in Asia and in Africa to reorganize the way they lived their lives and worked their land (see, for example, Shiva, 1991b). Vandana Shiva points to the violence wrought on people's livelihoods through the imposition of new technologies, and ultimately she links this to the rise in religious violence in India's Punjab, recounting how the Green Revolution, and its package of technologies and associated requirements, led to tensions between discontented farming communities – who demanded decentralization and an acknowledgement of their diverse interests – and the demands of uniformity and centralization led by the state:

> [The Green Revolution] is often credited with having transformed India from a 'begging bowl to a bread basket', and the Punjab is frequently cited as the Green Revolution's most celebrated success story. Yet far from bringing prosperity, two decades of the Green Revolution have left the Punjab riddled with discontent and violence. Instead of abundance, Punjab is beset with diseased soils, pest-infested crops, waterlogged deserts and indebted and discontented farmers. Instead of peace, the Punjab has inherited conflict and violence. (Shiva, 1991a: 57)

Shiva places her argument in the context of the development of an Indian, bottom-up 'Land Transformation' programme that would ultimately be shelved to make way for the 'New Agricultural Strategy', which concentrated on only a portion of arable land and was dedicated to supporting the new higher-yielding hybrid varieties, with their requirements for more intensive management, irrigation and application of fertilizer. Dependency on increased inputs (that were only initially subsidized), conflict caused by the installation of complex, centralized irrigation systems, and susceptibility to pests and diseases meant that yields were not as impressive as had been hoped. Over time, Shiva argues, the richer farmers were able to extract some benefit from the new crop varieties while the poorer farmers were faced with increasing indebtedness and demands to produce for urban markets. For Shiva, Green Revolution technologies ignited a set of ecological, social and political problems in the Punjab in ways that caused Sikh nationalism to flare up. The introduction of new, high-yielding varieties of crops had the most profound transformational effect on the Punjab. In adopting a technology we may be inviting far more than we bargained for – culturally, politically, economically, and in other ways. Shiva places the responsibility for the wide, multi-dimensional changes she describes squarely on the decision to introduce a 'modern' technological package from outside, as opposed to continuing to develop a 'traditional' local alternative. This 'cause-and-effect' technological determinism mirrors the stepwise modernization theory that underpins development. For Shiva, this external rupture tears at the social, political and ecological fabric of the Punjab and alters its future trajectory of development.

There is a lack of analysis of the complexity of the relationship between society and technology in many of the examples presented so far in this chapter. Technology is needed for economic development, or perhaps not needed from Vandana Shiva's perspective, and regardless of context technology is portrayed as deterministic; technology can transform society for the good, but often we need to transform society in order to best capture the benefits of technology. This makes the role technology can and will play in development seem almost inevitable. Thus modernization grossly oversimplifies the relationship between technology and society, by isolating a metaphor of 'change' from its context, which is partly a result of generating a series of context-less, people-less parables regarding the role technology has played in development in certain cases, such as those of the Asian Tigers or of Finland. The only measure of society in these cases is whether they are sufficiently or insufficiently knowledgeable about technology; there is little sense of the interaction of society with new technologies, and no sense of the roles of cultures, beliefs and traditions in shaping whether, and how, societies will use new knowledge and technologies. We also need to remember that changing technology is *always* only one factor influencing society among many others; technology's social effects are complex and contingent. Ulrich Beck in his *Risk Society* (1992) makes the case for 'reflexive modernization', part of which represents the idea that progress does not simply happen to societies; rather, society continuously comes to terms with progress, revising society's own version of modernity as it does so. Thus far, the depth and complexity of the interrelationship between society and technology has not been uncovered.

Black boxes and telecentres in Tanzania

Science appears to accumulate knowledge in a more or less ordered and progressive fashion. Science discussions tend to end with claims of solid knowledge or 'truths' more often than debates in other domains. These truths, facts or artefacts, can be thought of as 'black boxes', a term science and technology studies has appropriated from engineering that describes a stable 'input-output device', the inner workings of which do not need to be known for it to be used. 'Once a fact or artefact has become black-boxed, it acquires an air of inevitability. It looks as though it is the only possible solution to its set of problems. However, this tends to obscure its history behind a teleological story' (Sismondo, 2004: 97). In many ways we can see parallels between the black-boxing of particular scientific and technological facts and arte-facts, and the pre-eminence of development as the 'dominant problematic or interpretative grid through which the impover-ished regions of the world are known to us' (Ferguson, 1990: *viii*). Development discourses have coalesced to develop a 'regime of truth', an accepted way of describing and interacting with devel-oping countries or the 'Third World' (Escobar, 1995). These perspectives draw on the work of Michel Foucault in viewing development as a discursive field, or a system of power relations which produces ideas and truth (Foucault, 1979), which serve to 'black-box' development as something essential, the inner workings of which apparently do not need to be understood for it to succeed.

Rist (1997) argues that by coupling development and under-development, President Truman justified the possibility and necessity of intervention despite the fact that underdevelopment seemed to have no cause. The inertia of underdevelopment stood in sharp contrast to the vitality of the developed areas. Happiness could be delivered to the underdeveloped areas by the expanding and successful Western world through the application of its better technical knowledge and scientific rationalities (Abrahamsen, 2001). Thus we have a problem without a cause, and therefore a context with a solution that was thought to be contextless.

Ferguson (1990) demonstrates how contemporary develop-ment discourses have produced knowledge and institutions which support (and normalize) Western intervention in developing countries. That is not to say that development is not immune to

A telecentre in Tanzania

Claire Mercer (2005) shows how a modernization discourse that constructs the Internet as an inclusive development tool in Tanzania has become hegemonic amongst development agencies and telecommunication professionals. She shows how building a multi-donor-funded Multipurpose Community Telecentre in Mwanza Region, rural Tanzania, did not have the desired effect of allowing poor rural communities to have access to external markets and access to information for development. In reality 'communities' – at least not the poorest groups, most in need of assistance – did not avail themselves of the Telecentre. Rather, access to the Internet served as a means to separate out local communities into those who considered themselves 'modern' (and able to afford to use the facilities) and those who were not.

The Internet was not primarily used for business transactions or to seek knowledge for development but instead for emailing friends and relatives, reading news and sport. Given Internet-use data elsewhere in the world it is perhaps unsurprising that about a quarter of Internet use in Mwanza involved surfing for pornography. Internet use in the Telecentre mirrored use almost everywhere else in the world. This reflects Internet use in a whole host of other less-developed countries (see, for example, Miller and Slater, 2001).[10]

These usage patterns contrast sharply with the discourses on Internet technology and development that suggest that the Internet in Africa will be used for more productive purposes in pursuit of market-led development: 'in short, it is about Africa's need to advance along a technologically determined, linear path to modernity' (Mercer, 2005: 253). This speaks to a vision of Africa as devoid of the information and knowledge necessary for the development that would place Africa on the path to a future modelled on the 'information society'.

challenges and resistance. Attention has therefore focused on the ways in which development discourses have depoliticized these debates. Poverty becomes depoliticized by the 'hegemonic problematic of development' (*ibid*.: 256). A 'politics of truth' about the Third World and the need for development has been created through a 'historical construct that provides a space in which poor countries are known, specified and intervened upon' (Escobar, 1995: 45). What this means, in effect, is that decisions and judgements about what needs to be developed and how that development is to occur derive from the fields of knowledge that development generates. Identifying a series of absences – a lack of access to information technology, for example – delineates appropriate solutions, in this case the provision of access to information technologies. These narratives of absence or decay, and their counterparts of provision and development, are powerful rationalizing forces that drive development as the 'right' or 'only' means to obviate problems or push modernization.

What drives the idea that development is 'truth' is an overriding discourse powered by modernization theory, by the notion that societies must move from one Rostowian stage to the next and must do so by applying science and technology in an attempt to push development and economic growth. The Tanzanian telecentre project (see box) did three things. It presented a modern vision of Tanzania that did not chime with the reality: this represents a sort of African 'exceptionalism' that expects Africans to behave differently from Internet users elsewhere. Second, it delineated people into those who could both afford and operate the service and those who could not. Third, it framed rural Tanzania's lack of development in a particular antiseptic way: 'The problem of poverty is seen to arise not as a result of *exclusion* from global markets but rather due to a lack of engagement with global markets, and, crucially, a lack of *information* about global markets' (*ibid*.: 245). Mercer concludes that this development discourse suggests that Africa needs to play 'technological catch-up' with respect to Internet access and information technology, but has little to say about poverty or the root causes of underdevelopment in the first place.

Tissue culture bananas and the promise of *ex ante* studies

Tissue culture techniques utilize laboratory-based micropropagation techniques to provide disease-free planting material. The ability to utilize micropropagation techniques is a relatively simple but important first step in the process needed to produce genetically modified organisms, and consequently it is a technology that scientists in Africa have been keen to learn and put into practice. Theoretically bananas (*Musa* spp.) are one of the tropical crops most likely to benefit from tissue culture propagation, as the normal method of banana plant regeneration is to promote the growth and removal of suckers, a technique that aids the transfer of pathogens such as weevils, fungi and nematodes from one generation to the next. This is the technological premise behind an influential project aimed at promoting 'proto-biotechnology technologies' as the solution to a matrix of problems in East African agriculture. The project, Biotechnology to Benefit Small-Scale Banana Producers in Kenya,

> was developed in response to the rapid decline in banana production over the last 20 years. This decline was due to widespread soil degradation and the infestation of the nation's banana orchards with pests and diseases, problems further aggravated by the common practice of propagating new banana plants using infected suckers. The situation was threatening food security, employment, and incomes in banana-producing areas. (Wambugu and Kiome, 2001: *vii*)

The project creates a narrative about decline and projects a solution about growth and development by describing a series of seemingly interrelated problems (decline in banana production) and impacts (food security, employment, and lower incomes). The project rationale hangs on a series of big developmental problems in farmers' 'traditional' practice of using sucker material from diseased plants for micropropagation, thus spreading disease – and low yields – quickly from one generation of plants to the next. Tissue culture technologies are thus offered as a fix to multiple problems, and they must be transferred to farmers once they have been educated as to their benefits. Given the trappings of science described earlier, surprisingly few data are offered to support the arguments for crisis. The technology has been promoted heavily and supported by donors and partners, but given the large financial and institutional investments very little evidence exists for the success of the technology and its positive impacts on smallholders (Smith, 2007).

Studies from South Africa indicate that tissue culture banana yields may increase by 20 per cent in the first year, with a subsequent gradual decline to normal yields due to plants accumulating pathogens environmentally (Qaim, 1999).[11] The project conceptualizes problems and farmer behaviour in quite simple ways, when the reality of rural livelihoods is complex (Freeman *et al.*, 2004). The project is very focused on diffusing the technology, explaining to farmers why they must adopt it on the assumption that deficits in farmer knowledge are the reason technologies are not taken up. Traditionally, the uptake of agricultural technologies has been assumed to follow a sort of s-curve over time: initially a few innovators adopt a technology, then a bulk of people, then less people over time (Diederen *et al.*, 2003).

The other overriding narrative that stems from the project is the promise of future yield increases from the new bananas. This narrative revolves around the use of *ex ante* studies, economic analyses that model the future based on assumptions regarding uncertain variables. These studies project tissue culture banana yields over a set period. The projections are very optimistic. They assume all farmers adopt all the additional management practices suggested – which is an unlikely assumption and includes planting more tissue culture plantlets per hectare than normal plantlets which will obviously favourably skew data – and project yield increases for small-scale farmers of 150 per cent (Qaim, 1999). Given that the only peer-reviewed data suggest something akin to a 20 per cent increase in yield per annum this is a powerful claim for the technology. And it was never backed up with retrospective, *ex post,* studies of what actually happened in farmers' fields.

The project draws on a perceived history of yield decline to develop a projection of yield increases and makes use of economic tools to do so. *Ex ante* analyses are often used to project yield outcomes in relation to new agricultural technologies. The tissue culture case is an example of a project led by technology and not by demand. Consequently the project was obliged to frame the problem and the technology is particular ways. Bruno Latour talked of the act of 'projectization': any project is only likely to transmit information that will further the aims of the project and sustain it (Latour, 1996). More recently and in a developing country context this idea has been extended by David Mosse, who argues that one of the main goals of development projects is to generate policy-relevant ideas as this is what sustains them (Mosse, 2004). Ideas of progress are implict in all these ideas.

Hybrid maize, hybridity and diversity in Southern Africa

In moving away from understanding technology and its relation-ship with development as confluences of powerful discourses we

Green Revolution: from Rhodesia to Zimbabwe

The Green Revolution got under way in Zimbabwe – the then Federation of Rhodesia and Nyasaland – in 1960, a full five years before it did in Asia. A small research station had succeeded in developing its own hybrid maize, unimaginatively although patriotically named SR-52 (Southern Rhodesia 52), a type of seed that previously had emerged only from the modern laboratories of privately financed seed companies in the United States (McCann, 2005). This seed would have a profound effect not just in Southern Rhodesia but also in what would become Zambia and Malawi, with the result that those three nations would begin the twenty-first century among the world's top consumers of maize as human food.

Research on hybrid maize in the Federation began at the Salisbury Agricultural Research Station in 1932, with the first hybrid variety released to commercial farmers in 1949 (Mashingaidze, 1994). Maize breeders continued to develop improved hybrids throughout the 1950s and in 1960 they released SR-52. The combination of SR-52 seed, fertilizer and improved agronomic practices increased maize yields by 46 per cent over Southern Cross, the most common improved local variety (Eicher, 1995). In 1960, SR-52 had helped raised aggregate yields on commercial farms by more than 300 per cent over the previous decade. In 1950 only 22 per cent of the large-scale commercial farms in the region had planted hybrid maize; by the late 1960s more than 93 per cent were doing so, and it was nearly all SR-52 (McCann, 2005).

need to consider ways in which to ground our understanding of technology and development in real life, in local settings and interactions: how can we understand the relationship between technology and the people who use it? The ideas of diffusion, s-curves and knowledge deficit discussed earlier are inadequate in that they assume people behave only in certain ways. Instead we need to understand how people encounter technologies that may well have been developed in entirely different contexts and sometimes for entirely different purposes.

The roots of the hybrid maize variety SR-52 (see box) need to be traced far beyond the ingenuity of the Salisbury Agricultural Research Station breeders, to the initial monopolization by settler commercial farmers of the most fertile and well-watered lands of Southern Rhodesia. These farmers were to become a powerful lobby as they provided a steady economic and political base for the white settlers and their farming was heavily supported by investment (McCann, 2005). Early experiments in breeding took place in the context of a highly regulated system designed to support white commercial agriculture, which was constantly in danger of being undercut by African farmers who could produce surpluses more cheaply than settler farmers and consequently drove prices down. The Maize Control Board created government buying stations in settler farming areas, enforced a dual pricing system with higher prices for settler farms, restricted grain movement from Africa areas, and focused agricultural research into crop varieties – conducted principally by the Salisbury Agricultural Research Station – solely on the needs of settler commercial farmers. Like other, later Green Revolution crops, SR-52 rewarded intensive management, fresh seed each season, early planting, nitrogen fertilizer, irrigation and large-scale monocropping. Its adoption resulted in Rhodesia's commercial farms becoming globally competitive. However, without ready access to credit, inputs, and large tracts of well-watered land, SR-52 could be a risky undertaking.

Maize production became ever more important to Rhodesia with the collapse of the Federation of Rhodesia and Nyasaland in 1963 and Rhodesia's subsequent Unilateral Declaration of

Independence, which resulted in international trade sanctions against its export crops and industrial goods. Because maize was traded within the region it neatly side-stepped sanctions. However, discrepancies in maize sales and seed purchases uncovered the fact that African farmers had begun to purchase hybrid seed and were ready to invest in new early-maturing varieties which were of benefit to them.[12] In 1980, after the negotiated settlement to the guerrilla war, maize yields on African smallholder farms doubled and total production increased more than seven times in six years. By the end of the first decade of majority rule in Zimbabwe, almost 100 per cent of Zimbabwe's maize fields were planted with hybrids developed in the 1960s for commercial farms.

Meanwhile, Zambia, previously Northern Rhodesia, had travelled a very different path with a smoother transition to black majority rule and a relatively highly urbanized population. By the time the Federation ended in 1964 the hybrid maize revolution had taken hold in Zambia and farmers had begun to expand their growing areas. From the early 1960s until 1980 Zambia's maize farmers increased production by 400 per cent, expanding onto new lands, raising yields, and enjoying government subsidies for inputs. These changes were not evenly distributed, however. SR-52 was only adopted by around 30 per cent of small-scale farms; farmers simply could not meet the demanding management it needed to flourish, preferred not to monocrop, and were often too far from markets to compete. The fledgling Zambian government, which saw small-scale agriculture as a cornerstone of the country's economy, subsidized fertilizers heavily and, in order to stimulate production for urban residents, fixed pricing to compensate for the larger distances more remote farmers would have to travel to market. In effect, Zambia's National Agricultural Marketing Board had completely reversed the policy of its and Zimbabwe's colonial predecessors (McCann, 2005).

In the 1970s and 1980s Zambia's successes began to disintegrate for two reasons. First, local seed producers managed to contaminate its limited supplies of the vulnerable SR-52. Second, Zambia's stance on sanctions against Rhodesia, coupled with an initial decline in its economically vital copper mining, began to bite (Ferguson, 1997). Donors managed to reinvigorate Zambia's own hybrid maize research programme and in 1984 the previously moribund Mazabuke Maize Research Institute released MM752, which it claimed could outcompete SR-52 in terms of yield, quicker maturation and disease resistance. It seemed that Zambia had performed an agrarian miracle. However, the country's investment in agriculture had been underpinned by its income from copper. In the 1970s the crash of the global price of copper and its failure to recover, coupled with the turn towards a liberalization model by the International Monetary Fund and the World Bank, meant that Zambia could no longer support its agricultural sector as it once had. Loss of credit and price supports meant that many small-scale farms resorted to older, less market-oriented crops such as millet, groundnuts and sorghum (McCann, 2005). In the early twenty-first century the future structure of Zambia's agrarian economy remains unclear.

Malawi demonstrates another encounter with hybrid maize. Unlike Zambia and Zimbabwe, in Malawi the majority of maize comes from fields planted with other crops. This is perhaps not surprising given Malawi's lack of productive land and subsequent focus on densely settled, heavily cultivated plots. In these circumstances diversification of on-farm and off-farm income is the norm. Vulnerability often breeds a certain conservatism; farmers simply cannot afford the risk of experimentation and this partly explains why Malawian farmers were so much slower to adopt hybrid maize varieties than their neighbours. In addition, Malawian farmers preferred the tougher protective endosperm of their traditional varieties; they simply did not have the cash reserves to purchase new hybrid seeds and fertilizer each year, and they preferred the taste of their traditional varieties (Peters, 2002). By the early 1990s Malawi was catching up with its neighbours. The Ministry of Agriculture was making hybrid seed freely available and was supporting Malawi's breeders in developing their own hybrid varieties that displayed the taste and storage characteristics demanded by the local market while still retaining the early-maturing qualities that increased the chances of avoiding the failure of the rains. In Malawi maize was a food crop, not a cash crop linking the farm to a national economy. There simply was not the same early demand for innovation of hybrid maize in Malawi. Nevertheless, Malawi has gone on to produce its own locally suited hybrid maize varieties (McCann, 2005).

Hybridization does not refer only to the development of new breeds of crops. It is a post-colonial theoretical term that describes the reconfiguration of cultures as they interact, a process that is repressed within binaries such as 'Western/indigenous' or 'scientific/traditional' (Bhabha, 1994). The concept of hybridity does not represent a condition that exists between two binaries of purity or stasis; rather, it should be thought of as the enduring condition of all cultures (Rosaldo, 1995). There is nothing except the lending and borrowing between cultures of ideas, knowledge, artefacts and practices. In acknowledging hybridity we can no longer conceptualize development interventions and the development, promotion and adoption of technologies as a simple mimetic process whereby powerless and knowledgeless recipients adopt Western values, artefacts and practices. We cannot neglect the workings of power and therefore the dominance of the West when thinking about hybridity, but disparities of power need not and do not result in facsimiles (Erikkson Baaz, 2005). Rather, hybridity is unpredictable and context-bound, and from this perspective development and the impact of technologies associated with development do not imply an end of diversity but rather a site where 'new' diversities, other modernities and new technology/ society interactions are constantly being created.

SR-52 and its offspring illustrate hybridity in action. That a hybrid maize developed specifically for settler commercial farmers as the bulwark of a colonial state can end up playing a role in the nation building of a post-colonial Zambia and as a staple food in the multiple livelihood strategies of small-scale farmers in Malawi speaks to the local complexity of technology diffusion. S-curves do not seem to fit the pattern of constant negotiation and re-negotiation that has been played out across Southern Africa since 1960. Certainly, as the unexpected uptake of early-maturing hybrid maize by African farmers in Zimbabwe illustrates, it is not always possible to foresee what technologies will become, far less plan for it.

Conclusion

This chapter has set out to uncover some of the powerful narratives and dynamics that shape technology and development and identify perspectives that help us analyse and understand them. Modernization was introduced as an influential idea, which has shaped much thinking and policy regarding development, economic growth and the role of technological change, and the notion that 'progress' takes place in linear, singular ways.

The East Asian Tigers seemingly support modernization theory but on closer inspection they show that the way each country evolved was quite different. The case of the Tanzanian telecentre illustrates how powerful visions of modernity may be, blinding us not only to what people really want, but to what they really want to do. The tissue culture banana study showed how in letting science drive a project we can obscure the present and local in order to portray the past and the future in particular ways. Both case studies illustrate the drive and power of development narratives, and the desire to find a quick technological fix, perhaps as a response to the sheer enormity of the task at hand. Perhaps, in seeking to create a just, modern world as quickly as possible, it is only natural to reach for the possibility and potential of science and technology?

The hybrid maize case study presents a different perspective. Zimbabwe's SR-52 illustrated how technologies can be taken up in quite unexpected ways in different contexts – the result being a multiple reconfiguration of seed and agriculture. SR-52 illustrates something else, the benefit of investing in research and development and in concentrating research expertise in institutions. These ideas, of investment in agricultural research and concentration and institutionalization of agricultural research, have been discourses of science and technology for development policy since the Green Revolution. The next chapter will explore the post-war institutionalization and internationalization of research for development and its implications.

Further reading

Castells, M. (1998) *End of Millennium*, Volume 3. *The Information Age: Economy, Society and Culture*, Blackwell, London.

Commission for Africa (2005) *Our Common Interest. Report of the Commission for Africa*, Penguin, London.

Escobar, A. (1995) *Encountering Development: the Making and Unmaking of the Third World*, Princeton University Press, Princeton NJ.

Juma, C. and L. Yee-Cheong (2005) *Innovation: Applying Knowledge in Development, Taskforce 10*, Earthscan, London.

Power, M. (2003) *Rethinking Development Geographies*, Routledge, London.

Shiva, V. (1993) *Monocultures of the Mind: Perspectives on Biodiversity and Biotechnology*, Zed Books, London.

2 | The Internationalization of Science

In 1960, as the Salisbury Agricultural Research Station released its maize hybrid SR-52 to a target market of settler commercial farmers, the International Rice Research Institute (IRRI) was opened with a much grander remit: to 'solve this problem of rice' (Harrar, 1958 in Anderson, 1991). Although 1960 has been widely cited as the 'beginning' of the Green Revolution (Wade, 1974; Ruttan, 1977), its roots can be traced to technical assistance programmes introduced into Latin America in the 1940s (Fitzgerald, 1996). Nevertheless, 1960 is an important date as it denotes the institutionalization of the Green Revolution with the opening of IRRI in Los Baños in the Philippines. This institute, together with the research programmes that would eventually coalesce into the Mexico-based CIMMYT (Centro Internacional de Mejoramiento de Maíz y Trigo), produced the hybrid seeds and management innovations of the Green Revolution that would eventually lead to the development of a network of International Agricultural Research Centres (IARCs) as the dominant model of agricultural research in the developing regions of the world, and collective, public funding of research as the prevailing mode of supporting research in search of developmental goals.

IRRI and CIMMYT would form the basis for the Consultative Group for International Agricultural Research (CGIAR), which would become by its own account the single largest public investment into generating science-based solutions to the challenge of poverty eradication. Established in 1971 by international organizations, national governments and the Ford and Rockefeller Foundations, who sought to coordinate and support agricultural research for development, the CGIAR initially consisted of four research centres mandated with improving the yields of common staple crops in the agro-ecological zones of the developing world (IRRI, CIMMYT, the Africa-focused International Institute of Tropical Agriculture and the Latin America-based Centro Internacional de Agricultura Tropica). The rationale behind the CGIAR was that massive, focused funding of research institutes with defined agendas could supplement the relatively limited capacity of developing-country National Agricultural Research Systems (NARS) to undertake basic research. Today, the CGIAR is composed of 15 commodity-oriented, eco-regional centres for natural resource management, policy and capacity building. Its annual budget has expanded from an initial US$20.7 million in 1971 to US$425 million in 2004 (Alston *et al.*, 2006). The CGIAR was built on the conviction that scientific knowledge can promote societal change. Science and technology were seen as tools that could be wielded universally to deal with the major problems of the post-war era: food insecurity, political instability in Asia, and underdevelopment as a limit to the further growth of the developed countries. The technique was to replace 'traditional' varieties of staple crops and agricultural practices with their improved 'modern' counterparts.

The immediate post-war period also witnessed the institutionalization and internationalization of public health and health research. In 1948, the last of the newly founded United Nations agencies, the World Health Organization (WHO), was inaugurated. The WHO was doubly rooted in the post-war desire for peace and cooperation and a belief in the unifying possibilities of science. Health would serve as an international rallying point and the WHO's cadre of 'professional people' who approached their work with 'objectivity and scientific spirit' would form the heart of this endeavour.[13] The WHO was explicitly focused on health as opposed to disease and ambitiously envisioned good health for 'all peoples'. The WHO agenda would revolve around five functions: field operations, education, regulation of international conventions, research, and coordination of/cooperation with all organizations dealing with health. As it was clear that any one country could not deal with epidemic disease, countries were eager to cede power to the new institution. Initially the WHO was well funded, especially by the United States, and by 2006–7 the total annual budget of all WHO activities would amount to approximately US$3.3 billion, with funding coming from both donor and member states (World Health Organization, 2007). The WHO was highly technocratic and staffed by doctors and health professionals who soon cultivated an international *esprit de corps*. Above all else, the WHO grew to value professional competence and sought to develop a group of international health professionals who demonstrated the highest technical expertise. Such was the WHO's focus on employing people at the cutting edge of medical knowledge that staff were contracted for relatively short periods of time, as otherwise it would be exceedingly difficult to remain up to date with health innovations whilst in the field (Staples, 2006).

This chapter will examine the development of the often-contradictory paradigms of the institutionalization and internationalization of research for development in the post-war era. Development and scientific research for development were increasingly organized around large, international institutions and increasingly development was seen as a global endeavour to be led through and by international partnerships. This global, macro approach determined the ways in which development would take place, shaped the way in which science was used as a solution to developmental problems, and framed the relationship between science, technology and development. The roots of institutionalization and internationalization can be seen in the idea of modernization, but, as the case studies in this chapter show, the impacts of these processes were often unexpected and never uniform or linear. Of the case studies, the WHO is the epitome of international technical and scientific collaboration in health, the CGIAR a model of institutionalization that fundamentally shapes agricultural research in developing countries to this day.

The World Health Organization and the Malaria Eradication Programme

In 1955 the WHO launched the most ambitious public health programme ever attempted, the global eradication of malaria. Established as an agency of the United Nations only a few years earlier, the WHO believed that science could provide the means to accomplish the task and that, as an organization above politics and nation states, it was the ideal institution to lead the task. The Malaria Eradication Programme (MEP) was an immense project, involving the coordination of multilateral and bilateral donors, the support of national programmes and the creation of a world-wide infrastructure to generate and disseminate research, expertise and training (Staples, 2006).

At the time malaria killed more people than any other disease. It is a parasitic infection of the blood spread by female mosquitoes and is most prevalent in low-lying tropical and sub-tropical regions of the world, many of which are found in developing countries. Before the Second World War malaria annually infected 750 million people, caused around 7.5 million deaths, and contributed to unquantifiable lost productivity due to illness (Russell, 1952). Early attempts at dealing with malaria meant draining swamps to eliminate mosquito-breeding areas, or moving vulnerable populations. This clearly wasn't practical at a global scale and other treatments such as consuming quinine to control the onset of malaria were not very effective. Attention therefore turned to vector control, and chemists focused on insecticide development. The WHO, with its cadre of scientific and medical professionals and global remit, felt well equipped to deal with malaria on a massive scale. At about the same time, post-war advances in insecticide development cleared the path for WHO's plans. Dichloro-diphenyl-trichloroethane (DDT) was a long-lasting insecticide, effective for months with a single application. DDT's potency meant that relatively small teams of technicians could spray the interiors of dwellings once or twice a year to achieve a hitherto impossible level of mosquito control at low cost. If mosquito eradication was effective enough, the WHO had a vision of driving the malaria parasite into extinction – and DDT would be just the technology: 'Never in the history of entomology has a chemical been discovered that offers such promise to mankind for relief from his insect problems as DDT' (Rohwer, 1945: 144, cited in Maguire, 2004: 123).

This grand vision, of a relatively new organization achieving something global through science and planning, perhaps blinded WHO decision makers to early evidence suggesting there were dangers in the widespread and sustained use of a chemical as potent as DDT. There were reports of intensive applications of DDT killing birds, and less-intensive applications accumulating in water sources and killing aquatic wildlife. DDT's advantage, its potency and long life, was also a threat to the environment (Staples, 2006). As early as 1946 published research was indicating that DDT should be treated with circumspection, but the WHO pressed on regardless (Cottan and Higgins, 1946).

Within five years of the MEP being launched almost one hundred affected countries were undertaking WHO-led eradication programmes. The rapid spread of the programme was a

The Malaria Eradication Programme

Backed initially by United States funding, partially politically strategic, the WHO developed a programme of eradication to be implemented globally. A staged programme of initial research, education and new local legislation was followed by six-monthly spraying of housing for several years; once no new infections were observed for three years a long-term epidemiological sur-veillance phase would begin. This strategy was highly technical, organized and centralized. Based on a scientific standardization of methods, reporting and analysis, it required extensive training of professionals in the countries in which treatment would take place.

testament to centralized planning and mobilization of resources, but led to problems. Malaria in Africa proved much more diffi-cult to deal with as it was endemic owing to the climate and par-ticular characteristics of the mosquito vectors there. As contract-ing and surviving malaria in childhood conferred a degree of adult immunity, any Africa-wide programme had to focus on complete eradication and not just suppression if it were to be suc-cessful, otherwise potentially people would become more vulner-able to infection. Africa presented other difficulties: a poorer infrastructure than other affected regions, housing materials that would not take the spraying, and people who would simply refuse it. While other regions seemed to be able to eradicate malaria, transmission never ceased in Africa.[14]

Other problems arose. The highly structured spraying strug-gled with nomadic peoples, migrant workers and the like. Spraying was not always undertaken effectively. Not enough staff were available. The problem was that eradication had to be complete for it to work: as mosquitoes would eventually develop resistance to DDT, mosquito reservoirs of the malaria parasite had to be wiped out. Ultimately the task was too huge and increasingly complex, and resources too thinly spread. MEP member countries simply could not afford to be involved, and when health budgets were cut MEP activities were usually first to be slashed. The final reservoirs of mosquitoes were never reached (Staples, 2006). In 1969 the programme was closed down.

The MEP was in some respects a success: undoubtedly it saved hundreds of millions of lives, mortality rates tumbled, and an enormous global programme was mobilized quickly. However, it did not have the same impact across Africa, where half of all malaria infections occurred. There, it failed to persuade partner countries to invest in the programme in order to undertake the needed epidemiological surveillance, and they chose to spend their money elsewhere. Ultimately the MEP failed when opinion – and research findings – turned against DDT. Some risks had been known to the WHO since the 1940s, but new research underlined the risks of bio-accumulation, and the sustained risks in aquatic environments where the pesticide could reside long after spraying had ceased, and accumulate far from its original source (*ibid.*).

Throughout the MEP the WHO had chosen to interpret difficulties – regardless of the issue – as individual technical difficulties that required modifications in approach rather than a reappraisal of the tenets of the MEP. The prize of eradicating malaria was seemingly too great to be sidelined, despite the environmental and financial costs, and other risks. When the MEP finally ceased, the WHO, which had lost a certain amount of credibility through the experience, approached subsequent eradication campaigns, against polio and the like, with far more circumspection and analysis. The WHO also renewed a commitment to building national health systems that had adequate and sustainable resources, rather than ambitious WHO-led schemes.

The Green Revolution, institutions and modernization

The international agricultural research centres were conceived of as tools to drive the modernization of 'backward', subsistence agricultural practices towards a more 'modern', market-led future:

> We would suggest that there are two types of activity which make sense: first, activities which explicitly face up to the complex and interrelated problems of ignorance and tradition, and to seek to attack those problems; and second, isolable technical problems which are so important that their solution would find acceptance and application even under present circumstances. (Harrar *et al.*, 1952: 25–6, in Anderson, 1991)

Partly because of the utmost faith scientists placed in their ability to solve previously intractable agricultural problems, and partly because of the idea that modernization was a universal, universalizing process, great emphasis was placed on using existing expertise to solve isolable technical problems. This perspective involved removing the research process from its context not once but twice. First, a particular North American perspective on how to undertake agricultural research was proposed as a model for the approach, and, second, the problems themselves were to be solved out of context; the problem of yield was taken to stand for the problem of production and the problem of production was taken to stand for the 'world food problem'. Yields of rice and other crops had doubled in the past fifty years in the United States. As the causes of these increases were at the time well known, generating similar increases in other countries and contexts would simply be a matter of direct technical intervention.

The premise behind the Green Revolution was simple – to develop a series of conventionally bred rice, wheat and other cereal varieties designed to respond well to artificial fertilizer. These crop varieties initially came from IRRI and CIMMYT. The focus of researchers was straightforward – to breed varieties that respond well to inputs and release them to farmers. There was much talk at the time of eliminating hunger and poverty 'at a stroke' (Cleaver, 1972). The reality was different. Green Revolution technologies – the packages of improved seeds, increased fertilizer and extensive irrigation – had a dramatic impact on

---

HYVs: crops for the modern world?

High-yielding varieties (HYVs) of many of these crops were 'semi-dwarf' varieties, bred to exhibit the traits of shorter varieties in order to be able to support higher yields without toppling, and to focus the plant's primary photosynthetic production on live cell material as opposed to woody stem production, resulting in higher yields. A negative effect of this is the reduced protection against pests and diseases that woody material affords the plant. A further characteristic of HYVs that made them particularly suited to monocropping and more intensive forms of agriculture was their genetic and phenotypic homogeneity. As HYVs are generally crossed from two inbred lines (in order to increase the chances of exhibiting particular characteristics) they result in a genetically homogeneous hybrid. This has great advantages for management as it serves to homogenize the response of all plants to particular management practices, although it does greatly increase the rate at which pests and diseases can spread – whereas high genetic variation in traditional plants makes it less likely that all plants will be affected by specific pests and diseases. These traits of HYVs could promise increased yields, but also demanded that farmers alter their farming practices, in some cases dramatically.

agriculture. Between 1961 and 1985 cereal production in developing countries doubled (Conway, 1987). Yields of rice, maize and wheat increased steadily and progressively over that time period. It is difficult to attribute the impacts of individual facets of the technologies but Conway suggests that seed development, increased fertilizer use and improved irrigation are roughly equal in impact – and therein lies the nub of the problem (*ibid.*). The poorest farmers in Asia, and more particularly in Africa, did not have the resources to adopt the entire package of these technologies. Increased yields were almost exclusively concentrated in the fields of those wealthy enough to fully exploit the technologies (Glaeser, 1987).

The previous chapter explored how prevailing thought regarding development, technology and modernization shaped the way in which development practitioners perceived the world, and influenced the solutions they sought. This is especially apparent in the germination and development of the institutions that would shape the Green Revolution. There are many powerful discourses of 'traditional', 'backward' and 'nineteenth century', juxtaposed with 'modern', 'progressive' and 'twentieth century', that have influenced thought regarding agricultural research for development and the Green Revolution (Anderson, 1991; Fitzgerald, 1996; Cullather, 2004). The geopolitical agenda of the Green Revolution and the political, commercial and strategic interests behind agricultural science have been the subject of many recent studies (Marglin, 1996; Esteva, 1996; Perkins, 1997; Cullather, 2004). Rather less has been written about the scientific and technological agendas that have shaped how this research would happen:

> While some have argued that the technologies exported to developing countries are inappropriate, one might extend the argument by locating the inappropriateness in the institutional structures

and ideologies from which these technologies have emerged. (Fitzgerald, 1996: 457)

Modernization can be discerned in the discourses and rhetoric behind the new international agricultural research centres, but it is within the centres themselves that we can unpick thinking about how research should occur, in what directions science should be advanced, and in what ways technologies can transform the lives of those selected as needing help. The historical organization of research and development within a centre, indeed within the idea of building a centre itself, helps us understand how science and technology were supposed to provide agricultural development and at a stroke solve the problem of 'underdevelopment'.

The post-war period has brought a proliferation of the number of institutions concerned with research (Gibbons *et al.*, 1994). Many of these research institutions were modelled on earlier ways to organize research and only relatively recently have we begun to examine and develop new institutional arrangements for the organization of agricultural research (Hall *et al.*, 2001) and research for development more generally (Chataway *et al.*, 2006). Research institutions, embedded as they are in norms and ways of doing things, are slow to evolve and relatively conservative in their organization. In this context, institutions become places where discourses are produced, recorded and stabilized, and put into circulation (Escobar, 1995; Staples, 2006). As the case of the WHO demonstrates, institutions become important nodes that suture together expert knowledge and Western science with implementation in the less-developed regions of the world. Institutional practices such as training and the organization of disciplinary practices engender ways of working between people and how they perceive the world; these epistemic communities become important in order to generate, validate and diffuse scientific and development knowledge (Kothari, 2005; Nightingale, 2005). The generation of just such communities of research practice and the institutions within which they worked would profoundly shape research for development.

Creating an institution: rice research in Asia

IRRI was opened in 1960. Originally conceived of and financed by the Rockefeller and Ford Foundations, its explicit goal was 'improv[ing] the well-being of present and future generations of rice farmers and consumers, particularly those with low incomes', while less explicitly solving Asian food problems and allaying South Asian political and economic concerns (Anderson *et al.*, 1991; Cullather, 2004). IRRI's mission was to develop varieties of rice that would yield several times more than then-current varieties (Chandler, 1992). Scientists in the United States had achieved this over the previous fifty years, and there was confidence that applying similar techniques and approaches in Asia would yield the same results. The focus was to produce high-yielding varieties that would respond well to the generous application of chemical and natural fertilizers. There was a very clear focus on the intensification and modernization of production, and a focus on areas where intensive, mechanized, irrigated rice production already took place.[15] An explicit focus on improvements in rain-fed or more marginal productive areas would only come many years later.

The Rockefeller and Ford Foundations had prior experience of funding agricultural science initiatives in developing countries. In the 1940s Rockefeller had funded Norman Borlaug's successful research into developing new strains of wheat in Mexico. Moreover, Rockefeller had experience of setting up new research institutions. There was a genuine belief at the time in the universally beneficial applicability of science and technology. Effective solutions would only emerge in the form of new technology produced by scientific research:

> Rice research should be 'truly internationalized'; differences of language, culture, race, creed, colour and tradition 'must be rendered unimportant'. Rendering these differences unimportant, presumably in some central place and by some external and powerful agency, would be the only way to 'develop broad plans for long-range agricultural problems'. (Anderson, 1991: 73)

Initial thought was given to offering support to several existing national research centres in South and East Asia in a decentralized system of agricultural research, partly because relatively successful rice breeding programmes already existed in several Asian countries, notably Japan and Taiwan. This was fairly swiftly discounted in favour of supporting the development of a new international research institute working solely on rice. There was a feeling that a 'new' centre would offer several advantages and, anyhow, it was felt that no existing centre truly had the potential to serve as a foundation. In 1954 a paper prepared for the Board of Trustees of the Rockefeller Foundation set out reasons for the establishment of a single centre, including a sense that 'international cooperation in any field of science would be a good thing as it would contribute toward a common pattern of global living', and that the 'basic problems concerning rice are universal problems, which can be properly attacked in one central laboratory which would make the results available to all. Many of the really fundamental physiological, biochemical, and genetic problems are essentially independent of geography, and are certainly independent of political boundaries; so that these problems could effectively and efficiently be attacked in one central institute.' More important than this, 'it should also be possible to concentrate a high-powered and efficient international team of experts, supplementing each other and forming in total a more effective group than any one country can hope to produce' (Chandler, 1992: 2–3).

Probably of most significance in the above text was the belief that one centre could work independently of geographic and political diversity, and therefore was the most effective means to organize such research. Research and the development of new rice varieties was to be centralized and then disseminated. 'Internationalizing rice research' actually meant centralizing and decontextualizing it.

IRRI was conceived of as a United States-style agricultural research endeavour. Transplanting American approaches in agricultural research and modernization to Mexico through the Mexico Agricultural Programme had yielded some successes, certainly in terms of the increases in yields 'modern' varieties of wheat achieved compared to their traditional counterparts (Baum, 1986). When aggregated down to the farmer, however, it is clear that the farmers who adopted new technologies, and enjoyed the greatest benefit, were those who most closely mirrored the farmers American scientists were used to working with: modern, mechanized, with capital to invest (Fitzgerald, 1996). The programme was much less successful where the American model of agricultural progress did not fit Mexican conditions. It was not surprising, then, that IRRI's initial focus to an extent mirrored the experience of rice research in the United States (Anderson *et al.*, 1991). Key management and senior research staff were all US citizens, all of whom had been embedded in the US academic and research environment. There was a sense of applying science to a problem as a priority. Issues of disseminating any new varieties developed would devolve to national-level programmes. Extension was thereafter a distant process, of little or no concern to lab scientists in the early years. 'No matter what the environment, the Rockefeller Foundation asserted, making the technical solution available would result in desirable social changes without additional political effort' (Anderson, 1991: 72). The institute was to study and seek solutions for only certain parameters of rice production, and it would do so in relative isolation. The conceptualization of the new rice research institute as an 'international' centre for rice research was also a conceptualization of rice research as a supranational enterprise, devoid of a focus on national and local issues of context and dissemination.

It would fall to the National Agricultural Research Systems (NARS) to actively disseminate the new seed technologies to farmers. In this way dissemination, and communication with farmers, were devolved to individual countries. The products of rice research, how they were used and what their impacts were, were further distanced from IRRI; there was thus no direct mechanism through which IRRI could learn about the impact of its research. The impacts of IRRI's research would also be dependent on the capacity of NARS to multiply rice seed, distribute it, educate farmers about its benefits, and monitor impacts. The capacity of NARS to undertake these tasks varied across countries, and over time several NARS within IRRI's orbit would lose capacity through funding constraints, new policy priorities, economic decline and the like. Indeed, the lack of capacity of NARS in Africa was and continues to be a major obstacle to the ability of African countries to take advantage of new agricultural technologies. Furthermore, relying on NARS to undertake all dissemination of seeds meant there was no dialogue between farmers and scientists. Rather, there would be a linear flow of new technologies from international research institutions, to national agricultural research systems, to extension services, and into farmers' fields. Blockages in this flow would be due to 'ignorance' and 'tradition', not the mis-application of scientific solutions to technical problems (Anderson *et al.*, 1991). In this context it is not surprising that the better-resourced, more successful farmers benefited most.

As was the case in Mexico and in the United States, agricultural modernization revolved around increasing yields. Anderson *et al.* talk about the 'mental construct' of extracting low yields as a technical problem experienced in the different social, ecological and political realities of rice production across Asia, at a stroke rendering these differences 'unimportant' (*ibid.*: 40). Rice production in South Asia, let alone elsewhere, was incredibly diverse, encompassing not only the irrigated or well-watered growing zones that IRRI would focus on, but also poorly rain-fed, periodically flooded, mountainous and even saline environments. On top of this, culture, embodied not only in how rice is produced, but how it is consumed, is entirely local in character. Nevertheless, these concerns, and indeed others concerning international versus local views on the nature of appropriate rice research, were swiftly brushed aside. Rice breeding dominated IRRI's efforts and would ultimately shape IRRI's influence and global standing. Ultimately IRRI would be defined by the rice varieties it developed. IRRI's new rice varieties would be a symbol of science and modernization: 'It's something you can see. You can say, "well, go out and look at it". It did happen' (Forrest Hill, in Cullather, 2004: 227).

Since the 1920s scientists in South Asia had been working on creating improved rice varieties. Indeed, Japan and Taiwan had both conducted sizeable, and successful, breeding programmes. There was thus a critical mass of knowledge to build on and a rich resource of genetic stock to tap into. Early breeding successes in Japan and Taiwan had had little sustained impact on yields and IRRI, as a priority, was to focus on what was to be known as 'varietal breeding' (Chandler, 1992). The rice breeding programme revolved around two tenets. First, that a rice variety with as close to universal application as possible would stand the best chance of raising production. Second, that a rice variety that produced best under optimal conditions was also likely to

IR8: from field plot to paddy field

High expectations surrounded the launch of IRRI's first high-yielding variety, dubbed 'IR8'. Upon its launch in 1966, IRRI initially asserted that IR8 would be universally applicable. There was a clamour for the 'miracle rice' and it was perhaps released prematurely. It was not until two years after launch that the seed was finally certified. Scientists were aware of susceptibilities to disease. In addition, the grain was not robust, being prone to cracking and splitting (IRRI, 1966). There was a feeling at the time that IRRI was releasing IR8 primarily to satisfy donors, foundations and governments rather than farmers.

IR8 certainly demonstrated impressive yields in field trials, and it raised IRRI's profile considerably. Expectation was that rapidly and universally increasing yields would inevitably lead to a glut in the market and a collapse in prices. However, ten years after the launch of IR8 the production impact of IR8 was perceived as 'modest'.[16] Besides disease resistance and grain quality, IR8 and successive new varieties (which generally improved on single issues identified – such as grain quality or resistance to specific diseases – without dealing with the package of issues) did not enjoy the wide adaptability IRRI had hoped it would achieve. The first-generation new varieties were best suited to irrigated environments, and required extensive and precise inputs of fertilizer. IRRI's 1979 Long Range Planning Committee report highlighted another set of factors that limited impact, including institutional barriers, farmer aversion to risk, resistance to new ideas, and unsupportive development policies. These factors undoubtedly played a role in limiting impact, but the fact remained that the first generation of new varieties did not have anything like the range of ecological adaptability or management flexibility hoped for or initially mooted by IRRI scientists.

perform best under sub-optimal conditions (IRRI, 1962). These beliefs in part rationalized the decision to centralize research and led to the dominance of rice breeding activities within IRRI. All other research activities were subordinate to, and in support of, breeding. IRRI initially looked inwards to its strengths, the strengths of the breeders it had appointed, and the strength of faith in breeding.

There were sound reasons for assuming plant breeding could find an effective, universal solution to the problems of stagnant yields. The central focus was on producing ever higher-yielding varieties of rice that would respond well to the application of fertilizers. Indeed, some traditional tropical varieties of rice would respond so effectively to fertilizer that their heavy loads would cause the plants to collapse and the rice to rot in the paddy fields. Therefore, developing varieties of rice that would not collapse under their own weight was crucial. Semi-dwarf varieties of *japonica* rice with shorter, thicker, more stable stems had already been developed by Japanese, Taiwanese and American scientists in temperate regions. However, these plants were unsuitable to tropical regions, where *indica* species dominated. A second constraint on increased yields was the length of the maturation process of rice plants. Focusing on developing plants that would mature in the shortest possible time, preferably in less than 100 days, was seen as crucial in impacting upon yields. IRRI, through a series of ambitious statements, had raised expectation that it could produce high-yielding, quick-maturing varieties that would grow well in a broad spectrum of soils, latitudes and environments.

IRRI's early experiences in developing new varieties were somewhat disappointing, especially seen in retrospect and in the context of early hopes. The science proved problematic, more complex than initially hoped, and the ideal of producing universally applicable high-yielding varieties had to be re-thought. In addition, a set of unforeseen supra-institutional obstructions existed, in terms of policy, bureaucracy, and a lack of capacity in NARS that had not been seen as important. IRRI had a remit for capacity building – indeed, it was one of its three central priorities – but it would become clear that IRRI would have to develop new relationships in order to overcome these problems. It is clear, however, that IRRI initially chose to take a very narrow view of the problem of rice production. The problem and its solution were boiled down to a simple causal statement. Pinning hopes to the development of universally adoptable varieties meant the problem could be dealt with universally. IR8 and its siblings did and could significantly raise yields, but that was just not having an impact in the paddy, in the market or across the region. IRRI's original conceptualization of the problem was purposefully narrow and focused, but when the first generation of new varieties failed to live up to expectations, the conceptualization was revealed as too narrow and too focused.

If IRRI was to increase production – the thinking now went – perhaps it ought to focus on rice production in the more favourable environments. If, however, the broader aim was still to raise incomes and living standards (closer to the original goal of IRRI), then the focus needed to shift to improving production in marginal conditions. This new debate, this new critique, was important in that it prompted a shift towards *in situ* research, implying a broader demand for more diverse varieties. Over the years IRRI has shifted its focus and reorganized its research structure away from an 'American experimental station' (Anderson *et al.*, 1991: 73) towards a model that would take responsibility for technology transfer, work through international research partnerships, and focus research into diverse agro-ecological regions. The breeding programme would continue to dominate, swallowing half of the annual budget year on year during the 1970s and 1980s (IRRI, 1979) but breeding would take in a new research and institutional context aimed at ensuring rice farmers in all environments would benefit (IRRI, 1985: 21). By the 1990s IRRI had rethought the role of science:

> Each IRRI scientist works with colleagues in other disciplines – inside IRRI, in national rice research programmes, in other advanced institutions and laboratories, in sister international agricultural research centres, in non-governmental organizations, in the private sector. . . . Collaboration has many synergistic benefits – speeding the transfer of information and advanced research methodologies, shortening the time needed to solve problems, enabling scientific collaboration across political borders and economic barriers. (IRRI, 1992: 2)

IRRI was repositioning itself as a coordinating hub for collaborative rice research, rather than a hub of fundamental (or 'basic') rice research. Complex problems require complex institutional assemblages, complex partnerships and sharing of complex local knowledge – something that the original vision of IRRI had been unable to provide.

The International Livestock Research Institute and 'Mode 1' and 'Mode 2' research

The CGIAR, mindful that food security hinged not only on crop improvement, diversified in the 1970s and began to invest in, among other things, livestock research. In contrast to the experience of IRRI, two independent livestock research centres were set up: the International Laboratory for Research on Animal Diseases (ILRAD) in Nairobi, which was focused on livestock health, and the International Livestock Centre for Africa (ILCA) in Addis Ababa, responsible for livestock production research. It was hoped the two centres would be highly synergistic, although they soon developed distinct characters and developed along different pathways. ILRAD became a scientific research laboratory equipped to conduct immunological studies on two productivity-limiting livestock diseases prevalent in Africa – *theileriosis* and *trypanosomosis*. Its agenda was strictly confined to vaccine development against the two mandate diseases: 'Vaccines are a more sustainable way of controlling disease than vector control using insecticides or parasite control using drug treatments, which have contaminative, drug residue or drug resistance side effects' (ILRAD, 1992: 1). Underlying these aspects was an interest in emergent biotechnological techniques – a vaccine was considered 'the scientifically most "elegant" solution' (Chataway *et al.*, 2007b: 177). According to early predictions, the mandate diseases could be controlled within seven to ten years of the centre's establishment. This, however, would prove to be a distinctly optimistic forecast (Clark *et al.*, 2007b).

For decades, *trypanosomiasis* control has been attempted primarily through two routes – vector (tsetse fly) control and trypanocide drugs. The former has involved a range of approaches, from tsetse habitat clearings and the use of impregnated traps, to the widespread application of insecticides and the use of the sterile male technique. Indeed, in the early to mid-1980s 'the days of tsetse seemed numbered' (Torr *et al.*, 2005: 1). Large-scale spraying at ground and aerial levels had all but eliminated tsetse from large, previously infested areas of East, West and Southern Africa. This had given enormous benefit to livestock owners, many of whom were poor farmers. In addition a range of newer technologies such as odour-baited targets and cattle treatments seemed to indicate that the problem was showing every sign of coming under permanent control. However, what seemed a promising research trajectory began to fall apart due to changing donor priorities and research policy positions. This, combined with general economic decline in Africa, meant that considerable ground was lost. It was in this context that ILRAD embarked on a biological solution to the *trypanosomiasis* problem in the early 1980s: the development of a vaccine. However, development was hampered by antigenic variation of the pathogen and vaccine research efforts effectively ended at the International Livestock Research Institute (ILRI) around 2000. The focus of *trypanosomiasis* research at ILRI has subsequently shifted to the genetic characterization of trypano-tolerant cattle (Hirvonen, 2005).

ILCA, in contrast, emphasized the importance of adopting a holistic 'systems approach' towards livestock production, advocating interdisciplinary, contextualized and applied research. In contrast to ILRAD, whose activities were concentrated at its Nairobi laboratories, ILCA operated as a decentralized centre, with its headquarters in Addis Ababa and a number of satellite programmes throughout the continent. ILCA was envisioned as a 'concept' as opposed to a distinctly bounded research programme. Initially, the centre's agenda would be set according to the emergent needs of Africa's livestock systems and ILCA did not have a set of pre-defined research topics. Also central to the ILCA concept was the notion that a wealth of knowledge already existed on the improvement of livestock production in Africa; what was lacking was an appreciation of the context in which that knowledge was to be applied. ILCA, in contrast to ILRAD, struggled to gain acceptance within the CGIAR. The centres would merge in 1985 as the International Livestock Research Institute, with the expectation that the new centre would build on the comparative advantages of both the scientific excellence of ILRAD and ILCA's connections with African livestock keepers. This merger, while partially enforced by cutbacks in the CGIAR's budget, was probably ill-advised and premature (Winrock, 1992) and ILRI has not been able to exploit the comparative advantages as it might have hoped, hampered by the sheer complexity of the science of its vaccine-based research agenda and by its inability to combine more science-led and more systems-led approaches effectively in its work.

The contrasting perspectives of ILRAD and ILCA underline an important concept in science policy: that of 'Mode 2' knowledge (Gibbons *et al.*, 1994). This idea has been developed in recognition of the way in which knowledge production is beginning to

Table 1 Comparison of 'Mode 1' and 'Mode 2' institutions

Mode 1	Mode 2
Main objective is the production of knowledge	Problem solving is the main objective
Homogeneous, hierarchical structure. Traditional mode of organization in universities	Heterogeneous team and unstable social structure of production (task-oriented network)
'Pure' disciplines are the locus of new knowledge production and scientific recognition	Multi-disciplinary
Staging process of scientific development: from fundamental to applied research	Contextualization of research and the localization of research in new social spaces
Peer review system as the predominant form of assessment (research, career)	End of academic monopoly on assessment of research
Main target for diffusion of knowledge is journals	Diversification and de-institutionalization of knowledge-diffusion activities

Derived from Gibbons *et al.*, 1994

change; in the post-war period knowledge production has become increasingly context-driven, problem-focused and inter-disciplinary. It increasingly involves constantly changing multi-disciplinary teams working on specific problems relevant to the real world. This is 'Mode 2' knowledge. In contrast, traditional 'Mode 1' knowledge is more academic, discipline-based and initiated by the researcher. The work of Gibbons *et al.* is not meant as a cataloguing of types of knowledge production but as a general description of types of knowledge production and research. The focus of their work is on understanding changes in knowledge production in contemporary industrial society, and is pertinent because it describes ways in which science, technology and knowledge production may be better integrated into economic development. Table 1 represents how these two perspectives can be reflected institutionally. It is easy to see how ILRAD might be described as 'Mode 1' and ILCA as 'Mode 2', for example, or to see that different institutional cultures, values and investments can entrench research in particular directions, making change extremely difficult. These ideas will be expanded on in the next chapter, where we look at whether we can make technology work better for people.

Conclusion

This chapter has examined the role publicly funded international research institutions played in shaping technology for development in the post-war era. The WHO, through its MEP and other programmes, demonstrated an extraordinary ability to mobilize resources and organize technological interventions across a hundred countries. Nevertheless, for various technical and organizational reasons the MEP was ultimately deemed a failure. IRRI and CIMMYT were central in developing the short-stemmed, high-yielding cereal crops that helped boost mean yields across Asia in the 1960s and 1970s. However, those best placed to benefit were the richer farmers with access to irrigation, mechanization and the means to purchase the complete package of seeds and inputs.[17] The professional, international cooperative model of the WHO and the centralized, institutionalized organization of IRRI demonstrated a brash optimism and were also reflections of prevailing thought regarding science and its role in development and modernization: that a universal technical plan could eradicate malaria wherever it occurred, and that it was possible to 'solve the rice problem' by dealing with the seemingly tractable problems of production and yield outside of their context. The focus on 'isolable technical problems' did reap benefits, but they were not the universal benefits promised or anticipated.

As poverty, and health and hunger, have increasingly been seen as multi-faceted, the work of the WHO and CGIAR have changed. The WHO has focused more on strengthening health systems, and institutions like IRRI are acting less as centres and more as centres of research networks. The ways in which knowledge and technology are being accumulated, developed and transferred are changing; there is a realization that technologies need to be created *with* communities, not simply *for* them.

The internationalization and institutionalization of science for development reflect development thinking more broadly: organizations like the World Bank, the International Monetary Fund, the United Nations and the FAO stem from the same idea – that development, and science, are matters of global application regardless of local context. The WHO and IRRI did demonstrate that massive public investment in research could reap significant outcomes, and their enduring influence can be felt today in calls for 'centres of research excellence' in Africa by the Commission for Africa, for example, or in the centralization of efforts like the

Children's Vaccine Initiative and the Global Fund to Fight AIDS, Tuberculosis and Malaria (Muraskin, 1998). IR8 is still planted and consumed around the world, and more recently DDT has made something of a comeback. In 1996, when South Africa stopped using DDT, the number of malaria cases doubled, and in 2001 it made the 'horrible choice for our country' to start targeted spraying again.[18] Since then the WHO has recommended DDT as an alternative to impregnated bed nets in West Africa.[19] Whither progress?

This chapter highlights two issues. First, it underlines some of the problems science faces in articulating development problems and communicating with and responding to the needs of the poorest members of society. In the absence of an appreciation of how one can communicate with diverse communities in diverse contexts, it is exceedingly difficult to conceptualize what solutions might exist for almost hidden problems. Second, the chapter highlights the sheer complexity of developmental problems. As convenient as it would be to isolate problems and deal with them discretely, the reality is that everything is contingent and inter-related: science must conceptualize context, and technologies must be adapted to and developed for it. The next chapter examines some of the more recent shifts in how science and technology for development have been practised and organized with these two issues in mind.

Further reading

Anderson, R., E. Levy and B. Morrison (1991) *Rice Science and Development Politics: Research Strategies and IRRI's Technologies Meet Asian Diversity,* Oxford University Press, Oxford.

Conway, G. (1987) *The Doubly Green Revolution,* Penguin, London.

Gibbons, M., C. Limoges, H. Nowotny, S. Schwartzman, P. Scott and M.

Trow (1994) *The New Production of Knowledge: the Dynamics of Science and Research in Contemporary Societies,* Sage Publications, London.

International Assessment of Agricultural Science and Technology for Development (2008) 'Synthesis Report of the International Assessment of Agricultural Science and Technology for Development', Island Press, Washington DC.

Mosse, D. (2004) *Cultivating Development: an Ethnography of Aid Policy and Practice,* Zed Books, London.

Staples, A. (2006) *The Birth of Development: How the World Bank, Food and Agriculture Organization, and World Health Organization Changed the World, 1945–1965,* Kent State University Press, Kent.

3 | Making Technology Work for the Poor?

The previous chapters have shown how science has long been understood as providing technologies in a linear fashion: the theory of modernization predicts that societies will move forwards in a certain way; science leads to the development of technologies that lead to societal change; technologies move from the laboratory to the field station to the farm; traditional knowledge is replaced by modern, scientific knowledge as people become educated. It seems that the actual mechanism of change is less important than the notion that change will take place. What the various case studies have shown is that technological interventions in society rarely play out as they had been planned. Technologies are used in surprising or unforeseen ways, or technologies amplify existing societal inequalities, or technologies are simply ignored or misconstrued. It is apparent that we need to think about science and technology – about knowledge and how it relates to society – in new ways if we are to engender the sort of developmental impacts we hope science and technology can make in less-developed countries. By the 1970s it was clear we had reached some kind of 'knowledge impasse' with regard to technology for development. The Green Revolution had produced unexpected impacts and, as questions regarding its environmental sustainability and social equity emerged, the CGIAR style of 'science for development' came under scrutiny (Glaeser, 1987). Poverty is today acknowledged as more multi-faceted than food security alone, and thanks to the work of people like Amartya Sen, food security itself is no longer seen as solely a technical problem. Consequently, the hegemony of science as the sole repository of relevant knowledge to address such issues has also eroded. Donor priorities have shifted away from technical interventions towards social mobilization, and this involves thinking about issues like food security, health, energy and environmental issues in concert. The 'technology for development' agenda is becoming increasingly complex (Leach and Scoones, 2006). Moreover, the liberalization of economies has led to a withdrawal of the state from its traditional areas of activity – including agriculture – and new actors, the private sector and civil society among them, have begun to fill the void. In addition, new technologies, often under private ownership, are reshaping the practice of research and raising questions about the most appropriate arrangements between public and private stakeholders. We are being forced to think about science and technology in these shifting policy, institutional and developmental contexts, and this involves thinking about poverty and development in more multi-dimensional ways; about the interrelationships between actors, institutions and sectors; and about the knowledge flows that allow these emerging complex assemblages to function – to develop, we hope, better and more appropriate technologies for development. Fundamentally this means we need to reflect on and problematize what we mean by 'knowledge' – whether it be 'scientific', 'traditional' or some other kind – and how it can forge interrelationships or drive them apart.

This chapter discusses new thinking regarding knowledge and knowledge production, and in doing so shows how understanding knowledge better allows us to develop institutions and networks more capable of shaping technologies for development. A key message is that knowledge need not only be thought of as subjectively valuable, but as something inherently valuable to be learnt, shared and experimented with. In exploring these issues it will become apparent that many new ways of organizing science and technology for development are not antithetical to the modalities employed in the immediate post-war development era. Instead, they cast them in a new light and in doing so point to ways in which new partnerships and new knowledge bases can forge more effective technological development – and development itself.

Thinking about a 'knowledge impasse'

It is clear that we need to find new ways to think about knowledge if we are going to be able to move beyond notions of 'transfers of technology' and assumptions that we can treat complex problems related to poverty and development as isolable and without context. Science and technology studies reminds us that science should not be set apart from other forms of knowledge. Latour (1987) has pointed out that 'rationality' is far too mysterious and 'thin' a notion to be useful in accounting for differences between scientific and non-scientific knowledge systems. In the 1960s and before, 'indigenous' was generally taken to mean 'traditional' and therefore backward, inefficient and something to be replaced. However, since then, presaging or at least occurring in tandem with a broader development shift towards 'participation', considerable attention has been paid to 'indigenous' knowledge.[20] Rather than being seen as an obstacle to development, to be overcome, indigenous knowledge was recognized as something to be tapped into and used, something that could, for example, be useful in developing better agricultural systems. This reformulation represented something of a break with the centralized, technically oriented solutions that had not had the hoped-for sweeping benefits for poor farmers and others. A new focus on indigenous knowledge was in part a reaction to large-scale scientific endeavours such as those described in the previous chapter, but it would be a mistake to assume this new focus was an outright rejection of modern science. In part it reflected a broader move away from the grand theories of development towards interventions that were more place- and time-specific. For example, more power was accorded to NGOs to undertake development, as the state in many developing countries was becoming less and less able to play a central role, and international organizations often did not have the local contacts and expertise necessary to work effectively in specific contexts and at small scales (Cernea, 1988).

Indigenous knowledge is often conceived of as something quite distinct from scientific or Western knowledge:

> Modern scientific knowledge is centralized and associated with the machinery of the state; and those who are its bearers believe in its superiority. Indigenous technical knowledge, in contrast, is scattered and associated with low-prestige rural life; even those who are its bearers may believe it to be inferior. (Chambers, 1980: 2)

The idea of a hierarchy of types of knowledge may be reflected onto processes of institutional change within research organizations. Both IRRI and ILRI illustrate the tensions between knowledge systems, in IRRI's case that of 'rice breeders' as the dominant group of researchers and in ILRI's case the notion that vaccine research was inherently more attractive or exciting than other avenues of research. How we perceive knowledge, as 'truth' or otherwise, as scientific or indigenous and so on, fundamentally shapes how we interact with it. In this interaction there is a risk that we create artificial boundaries, and in seeking to subvert perceived boundaries we delineate new hierarchies – for example that in some way indigenous knowledge is more 'honest', 'feminine' or 'in tune with the environment'.[21] Statements of this nature may well be true, but it is more useful to assess claims such as these on evidence rather than on any perceived genealogy of the knowledge itself.

Much of the practice of creating dichotomies between scientific and indigenous knowledge can be traced back to anthropology. Lévi-Strauss[22] has been enormously influential in suggesting that 'primitive' or traditional cultures are more deeply embedded in their environments than modern cultures, that 'primitive' peoples are less prone to analytic reasoning than their scientific counterparts; and finally that 'primitive' systems of thought are more 'enclosed' than scientific systems of thought. Consequently, by extension indigenous knowledge helps us understand context, whilst scientific knowledge helps us see the big picture; in other words the utilization of indigenous knowledge is concerned with meeting the necessities of day-to-day life, whilst scientific knowledge aims to construct generalizable explanations and is in some way removed from day-to-day life, and so is more likely to achieve transformational breakthroughs for society. In reality it is no more possible to divorce the exigencies of 'modern' life from science, than divorce 'traditional' life from experimentation and innovation. Blaikie (1985: 2), in placing the 'land manager' at the centre of his analysis to show how rural people best juggle their resources to operate within the constraints of political and economic systems, highlights local innovation in a broader context. In a similar vein, Richards (1989) talks of agriculture as a 'performance', continually played out and refined in the face of shifting contexts and demands. Agarwal (1995) shows how the 'artificial divide' between science and indigenous knowledge looks increasingly tenuous when we consider and compare agro-ecology and the multiple tree-cropping systems of smallholders in many parts of the world, or agronomy and indigenous techniques for the domestication of crops.[23] Ultimately it is in change, experimentation and transformation

Small is beautiful: the appropriate technology movement

An offshoot of the historical tensions between 'scientific' and 'indigenous' knowledge has been the 'appropriate technology' movement. This philosophy is slightly tangential to the main thrust of this chapter but the main ideas underpinning it, that technology ought to be designed with special consideration to the ethical, cultural and social aspects of the community it is intended for, are as relevant today as they were in the early 1970s. There is a sense that an appropriate technology should be the simplest possible means of accomplishing the particular task it is designed for, and therefore is of particular relevance in the context of developing countries or in rural settings. Schumacher's book *Small is Beautiful* (1973) was particularly influential in shaping these ideas, arguing that permanence would be the natural result of the development of simple, appropriate technology. As a general philosophy appropriate technology offers perspectives few people would argue with and provides a relevant critique of inappropriate technological development, especially if it were to provide a set of principles to which we could all aspire. The fact that it is most often suggested as the most appropriate approach for the poor, and people in developing countries, is slightly problematic, however, as it risks cutting off a whole range of other possibilities. Who is to decide what is 'appropriate', anyway, and seemingly complex, hi-tech 'inappropriate' technologies, appropriately applied, may make significant and sustainable developmental impacts. Schumacher intended his book to speak to all of us, regardless of personal circumstance, and this message risks getting lost in the matrix of values we attach to knowledge, instead becoming a means whereby solutions for one group of people may be proffered by another with little meaningful contextual engagement.

that the dichotomy between Western/scientific and traditional/ indigenous knowledge disintegrates. The dichotomy between science and indigenous knowledge sought to separate and pin down what has evidently continually transacted and evolved through contact, exchange, learning, and the adoption and use of technologies (*ibid.*).

Table 2 illustrates something of a convergence of scientific knowledge and indigenous knowledge. The reason, or the 'blame', for the failure of technological interventions has shifted from the shoulders of the farmer to those of the scientist. Quite apart from highlighting the sheer relativity of knowledge, this change has come about through a combination of the realization that technologies were not being taken up or having the impact that was intended, that farmers' knowledge was also valid and could help understand complex systems, and finally that it was impossible to improve and refine knowledge and technologies continually through a linear, one-way system. Modes of interaction had to be built into extension systems, otherwise there was simply no way to understand what was going wrong, right or indifferently with technological interventions. The convergence of these practical, conceptual and institutional dynamics had led to a complete reversal of 'blame'. However, whilst in the 1950s and 1960s only scientific knowledge mattered, in the 1990s it was not the case that only farmers' knowledge mattered. It was simply a dawning of the realization that all knowledge may 'matter', contingent on context, perspective and utility.[24]

This acknowledgement of the importance of knowledge in context also uncovered an appreciation that those very contexts were also explanatory factors in understanding why technologies worked or did not. The work of 'political ecologists' such as Piers Blaikie, and latterly Michael Watts and Richard Peet, was key in placing farmers, and human–environment relationships more broadly, in their proper political-economic context.[25] This

Table 2 The evolution of research and extension

	Explanation of farmers non-adoption	Prescription	Key extension activity	Socio-economic research	Dominant research methods
1950s 1960s	Ignorance	Extension	Teaching	Understanding the diffusion and adoption of technology	Questionnaire surveys
1970s 1980s	Farm-level constraints	Remove constraints	Supplying inputs	Understanding farming systems	Farming systems research
1990s	Technology does not fit	Change the process	Facilitating farmer participation	Enhancing farmers' competence	Participatory research by and with farmers

Derived from Chambers, 1993: 67

concern with the political economy of agrarian change cast rural people in an endless struggle to sustain themselves in the contexts of constraint and a lack of access to resources. Adopting or rejecting a technology was never simply a matter of not holding sufficient knowledge necessary to decide to use it, but was the result of a complex working out of risk, opportunities and costs.[26] The 'success' of technologies, what they represent, and whether they are adopted or not, was bound up in far more complex interrelationships than those suggested by the 'deficit model'. Technologies are not neutrally transferred from laboratory to field; their adoption, refinement and innovation are rather the result of complex interactions between different knowledge bases and perspectives, and linkages between different actors and organizations, all bound up in shifting contexts of risk, benefit, constraint and utility. This presents a far more compelling sense of how technologies come into being, and how they may benefit poor people and drive development, than that which drove the Green Revolution and other earlier endeavours.[27]

Collaborative research: mother and baby trials

Another of the CGIAR centres, the International Crops Research Institute for the Semi-Arid Tropics (ICRISAT), in collaboration with local NGOs, has developed several innovative, participatory research methodologies. One of these, 'mother and baby trials', has been widely adopted as a means to better understand how and why farmers invest in some crop management options and not in others, and how this information can be used to refine and implement more appropriate technological developments collaboratively. The approach was developed as part of a project aimed at supporting poor, female-headed households, generally the poorest and most vulnerable with least access to land, in developing more effective soil and crop management practices in Southern Africa. The methodology was developed from the premise that, even though there has been a greater emphasis on on-farm research and experimentation, appreciation on the part of scientists of farmers' real needs and priorities is often still inadequate. Research still rests on the assumption that productivity and profit are the key priorities for poor farmers, when in fact agricultural practices that require little labour or smooth seasonal shortfalls may be preferable, for example. Management options must therefore fit within the resource constraints and investment priorities of the poorest farmers.

Mother and baby trials: 'natural birth' for new technology?

The 'mother and baby trial' approach provides a way to connect assessment of technology by farmers – and therefore an implicit assessment of their technological wants, needs and priorities – with a biological assessment of technological performance in the field. The methodology has two stages. Firstly, the 'mother trial' takes place on-site, in the community, to test a range of hypotheses regarding technologies. This trial is initially managed and monitored by the researcher. The second stage, a series of 'baby trials', comprises a number of sub-sets of the mother trials. These baby trials are under farmer management and crucially use farm resources. This allows an analysis of the appropriateness of any given technology from the perspectives of both the farmer and the researcher. Each trial compares a sub-set of those tested in the mother trial and chosen either by the farmer or as a result of farmer–researcher consultation. Researchers advise on technological management and monitor progress and actual farmer practice. This dual trialling system allows detailed monitoring and evaluation of crop response via the mother trial, and systematic evaluation, by and of the farmers, of particular combinations of variables through the baby trials (Snapp et al., 2002). Furthermore, it builds trust, dialogue and participation between researcher and farmer, exposes the farmer to new technologies and practices, and provides an important qualitative element to the more tradition-ally qualitative field-trial-based research. Farmers' ranking of technologies and practices is combined with quantitative data and regressed in order to cater for variances in environmental conditions. In this way the trials attempt to overcome the dichotomy of seeking an understanding of local context whilst needing also to understand the broader productive potential and uptake of the technologies being tested.

Thinking about innovation

Allied to the increasing appreciation that 'indigenous' (or local) knowledge was important in situating technology has been a growing concern that the transfer of technology model did not actually reflect how innovation took place. In reality innovation interacts with economic production through a complex process that is intrinsically systemic and decidedly 'non-linear'. This perspective has grown in influence since the 1980s, particularly in developed country technology and industrial policy. It possesses considerable insights for developing countries too. Rooted in evolutionary economics, the argument runs that technical change is not characterized by processes of refinement and optimization over time, as neoclassical economics would suggest; rather, the characteristic features are learning and continuous change (Nelson and Winter, 1982). While most of the work on innovation systems has focused on developed country industrial economies, where the notion of a 'National Innovation System' emerged,[28] more recently the idea has been used as a means to analyse agricultural technology policy in developing countries.[29]

A National Innovation System can be described as the system or network of public and private sector organizations whose interactions produce, share and use economically useful knowledge. The component parts of the system, and how they interact, are shaped by their institutional settings: for example, professional norms within organizations, cultural norms more broadly, historical patterns of institutional development and national priorities (Clark *et al.*, 2003). These institutional settings are shaped by borders, economies and policies. It is not necessary for national governments to have purposefully shaped innovation systems in this way, but nations in which such interactive systems have (or have been) successfully developed display strong innovative performance. This has often been related to rapid rates of economic growth: to varying degrees, the Asian Tigers are good examples (Freeman, 1987). The idea of innovation systems does not present a policy blueprint for reform but instead is concerned with mapping and evaluating channels for knowledge flows, identifying bottlenecks in these flows, and suggesting appropriate remedial action. The work of Gibbons *et al.* (1994) can be seen to tie in closely here. In this sense the concept of innovation systems is really a metaphor for thinking about the innovation process, how it works, and how it can be encouraged to work better. This approach allows the agricultural sector, for example, to be viewed in a much more holistic manner. It allows us to visualize the full range of organizational forms and institutional settings that actually make up the technology system. This might include stakeholders who are not so evidently part of the linear system of transfer of technology – NGOs or farmers' interest groups, for example.[30] This broader conceptualization allows us to place the public sector in a broader context and in doing so to identify what its most appropriate role in encouraging innovation might be. It also allows us to identify the types and strengths of linkages and partnerships that have become important within the system, and accordingly identify the types of systemic failure that may constrain otherwise productive relationships. Finally, such an approach allows us to explore the agendas and aims of different stakeholders in the system (Clark *et al.*, 2003). The innovation systems approach, then, provides a conceptual tool to help us think about the types of policy frameworks, partnership arrangements and organizational approaches that can best lead to the innovation of new knowledge and technologies. It ties neatly into debates regarding how we attribute value to knowledge and understand knowledge to work, and provides a sharp critique of the earlier transfer-of-technology approaches and their focus on the primacy of scientific knowledge, on the one hand, and 'knowledge deficits' to be overcome on the other. Hall (2007: 2) has boiled the concept down into three broad principles:

> (1) Innovation requires knowledge from multiple sources, including from users of that knowledge; (2) It involves those different sources of knowledge interacting with each other in order to share and combine ideas; and, (3) These interactions and processes are normally very specific to a particular context, and each context has its own routines and traditions that reflect historical origins shaped by culture, politics and power.

Innovation and treadle pumps in Bangladesh

In 1984 an India-based international NGO, International Development Enterprises (IDE), identified treadle pump technologies of seemingly great potential for Bangladesh.[31] At the time Bangladesh had recently suffered extensive flooding, which had damaged productive potential – and, paradoxically, ready access to water had become a particular constraint. Some pump technologies existed in Bangladesh but were not of sufficient capacity for agricultural use (hand pumps), too expensive for poor farmers to use (diesel and electric pumps), or not readily accessible (well pumps). The treadle pump offered a compromise solution as a foot-operated device that uses a flexible tube to pump water from shallow aquifers. It was cheap, efficient and simple, costing less than $25 for purchase and installation.[32] This was considerably cheaper than other options. Once IDE had, with farmers, identified the treadle pump as the preferred technology it began to analyse why the device had not penetrated the market previously. IDE had set itself the target of establishing a viable supply chain for the technology. Between 1984 and 1989, IDE played the role of direct service provider, demonstrating the technology, providing technical assistance to partner producers, establishing quality control and selling treadle pumps with a relatively small margin. Following this initial start-up phase IDE played the role of market facilitator, deliberately withdrawing from the direct sales function and instead seeking to establish a private supply chain. IDE provided technical support to a large number of small treadle pump fabricators who had developed within several Bangladeshi markets. The period between 1990 and 1995 was coined the 'KB Phase'. During this period IDE established and managed a company called KB (short for the brand name, *Krishak Bandhu,* meaning farmer's friend). Since 1995, IDE moved to a broader phase where it promotes the idea of the treadle pump in general through training and facilitation. Since 1984 IDE has sold almost 1.5 million units in Bangladesh (Clark *et al.*, 2002). Over this period the project was funded by donors to the tune of $8–10 million.

IDE's experience with the treadle pump in Bangladesh highlights four pertinent issues. First, it underlines the complexity inherent within even relatively simple technologies such as labour-assisted pumps. Many forms of different designs, materials and fabrication processes shape not only the pump but also the relationships and activities of the many organizations who interact to develop and market it. There is little sign of linear technological development in this case. Second, the case represents an insightful study in technology development as a managed process. IDE conceived of the innovation (in the context of Bangladesh at least) and then orchestrated its introduction and uptake through a series of linked activities, whilst all the time seeking to make its own role in the value chain redundant. By promoting interest and capacity in partners, IDE sought to build sufficient momentum for it to withdraw without impacting upon the quality and supply of pumps. Third, the case emphasizes the fundamental importance of user interaction. Treadle pump technologies diffused rapidly in part because close attention was paid to farmer needs. In addition, IDE was initially successful in supporting small businesses to develop and market the treadle pump themselves; this competition led to several incremental innovations that lowered the price. This highly interactive, competitive environment provided the stimulation IDE's partners needed to adapt and market the pump successfully in the Bangladeshi context. Finally, and perhaps most importantly, the IDE experience underlines the importance of building long-term capacity amongst partners. IDE was careful in staging its interactions with the treadle pump in such a way as to build initial capacity in fabrication, assist with marketing, develop a learning environment and promote the technology more broadly – all the while gradually withdrawing. It should be noted that this process occurred over some eighteen years, a far longer period than most donors would contemplate funding individual projects for.[33] Engendering innovation, learning and impact is a far more involved and complex process than that, but it can reap rewards.

Mobile phones, fishermen and farmers' markets

Thinking about technological innovation in a more systemic way forces us to think more carefully about the role of markets in shaping and providing technology for development. First, we can think about the role technologies can play in making markets more efficient, in strengthening the position of less developed countries in global markets, and in providing access to market information. There is enormous debate on the extent, or even the existence, of the 'digital economy' (McNamara, 2003) and it is tremendously difficult to unpick the role technologies and technological development play in the economy, or even in sectors of the economy, as technology is so embedded in all economic activity, even in the least-developed countries. There is much debate about the role technology can play in markets, and the varying notions of a 'network society', 'flat world' and 'digital age' are powerful metaphors. The *UN Millennium Report*, for example, speaks about ICT in the following terms:

> ICT is pervasive and cross-cutting and can be applied to the full range of human activity, from personal use to business and government uses. It allows people with access to networks to benefit from exponentially increasing returns as network usage increases. It fosters the dissemination of information and knowledge by separating content from physical location. (Juma and Yee-Cheong, 2005: 49)

This is a powerful statement, but pretty vague in terms of how, concretely, ICT will aid development. Indeed the report is more circumspect elsewhere, noting that 'anecdotal claims about the impact of ICT on development need to be accompanied by strong methodological and conceptual foundations' (*ibid.*: 48). A specialist report on ICT for development underlines that 'poverty and low growth remain seemingly intractable problems . . .

Catching up – with a mobile phone ...

Mobile phone use is probably one of the best examples of the ways in which developing countries can play 'technological catch-up' with developed countries. For many people in sub-Saharan Africa their first taste of owning a telephone will be a mobile phone. This would have been inconceivable in developed countries even a few years ago. It is easier to install the infrastructure required for mobile phone technologies than wired phones, and – as private sector telecommunications companies can and do make a profit in even relatively poor countries – the spread of their networks will widen.[34] Mobile phones are likely to become the ICT of choice in countries that do not already possess extensive wired telephone networks.

... or a mobile bank

As well as giving access to market information, mobile phone technologies may facilitate the creation of new markets. Mobile banking, or M-banking, is gaining currency in countries as far apart as the Philippines and Kenya. In Kenya, in particular, M-PESA, a mobile phone application that allows users to send small amounts of money to other mobile phone users via a nationwide system of agents who handle the physical money, is becoming very popular. In Kenya M-PESA is playing an important role in facilitating the transmission of resources between rural-urban households, a common form of household in countries where household members are obliged to migrate to cities in the hope of securing work and remitting money and resources to their rural family. Formerly, sending money and resources home has been complicated and relatively expensive as poorer households do not have access to formal banking systems and had to rely on informal means such as sending money via go-betweens using public transport. M-PESA appears to be creating stronger and more tangible financial ties between such dual-location households, and in doing so provides new and more stable flows of money to underdeveloped rural communities in Kenya, allowing rural households to manage their resources better. M-PESA is thus generating a new flow of capital for rural households and communities, strengthening an income stream which otherwise can become very tenuous.[35] M-PESA is being looked at as an application for neighbouring countries in East Africa and discussions are under way about setting up an international service which would aid the relationship between African diasporic communities and their families back home. M-banking is an example of a technological solution that meets a definite developmental need.

because ICTs themselves have not proved to be the transformative tools that some had predicted they would be' (McNamara, 2003: 3). There are many positive examples of the impact of ICT in markets, but they are small-scale, although perhaps nonetheless important for that.[36]

Much research shows that access to information and communication technologies, in particular mobile phones, enables farmers to engage with market information from a position of strength. Research among fishermen in Kerala State, India shows that since the introduction of a mobile phone network in 1997 the number of fishermen who travelled beyond their usual markets to sell their fish elsewhere jumped from zero to 35 per cent. Mobile phones, in providing the fishermen with better access to market information, also helped eliminate wastage and 'smoothed' prices across local markets – indicating that the broader market was working more efficiently, and presumably meaning that people in less-accessible markets were not being disadvantaged unduly in having to pay higher prices (Jensen, 2007). Experiences among farmers in Tanzania also suggests that mobile phones allow them to access information regarding wholesale prices. Instead of consigning produce blindly, they are able to choose between local markets or markets in Dar es Salaam (Molony, 2008b). Similarly, research on grain traders in Niger suggests that the major impact of mobile phone use amongst traders was a reduction in the time and cost associated with searching for better prices. Mobile phones were giving access to market information for a greater number of markets over a far wider area (Aker, 2007).

While evidence suggests that mobile phones allow farmers, fishermen and other traders to gain information regarding market prices, and thus become more competitive, there is much less compelling evidence that mobile phones build new networks – personal, professional or otherwise. Even M-banking helps to strengthen existing relationships of obligation as opposed to creating new relationships. Research on customer acquisition and retention in urban India (Donner, 2007) and on agricultural marketing of perishable foodstuffs in Tanzania (Molony, 2008b) both suggest that face-to-face interaction remains the basis of 'real' networking, interaction and negotiation. Technologies such as mobile phones are playing an important role in local markets and designing supportive policies to encourage their wide and cheap availability seems like a simple, yet effective intervention. Little empirical evidence, however, suggests that ICTs are having the transformative effects at the level of national and global markets that have sometimes been promised.[37] That of course does not mean their impact will not multiply in the future as technologies, and indeed markets, evolve and change.

Markets, incentives and the private sector

Next, and more broadly, we need to think carefully about the roles markets and the private sector play in developing and disseminating technologies to those most in need of them. Past efforts to promote technology for development were based largely on a public sector model. The Green Revolution, with the subsequent development and support of the CGIAR system, is probably the best example of this, where a combination of international, national and philanthropic funding created international research centres to support the poorly funded NARS found in many less-developed countries. Until relatively recently nearly all medical innovations were developed in publicly funded universities and laboratories.

We are currently witnessing an enormous shift in the balance of power of research and development. In agriculture, the five largest technology-led multinational companies – Bayer, Dow

Agro, DuPont, Monsanto and Syngenta – spend $7.3 billion per annum on agricultural research. That is more than twenty times the budget of the publicly funded CGIAR system (which remains the largest-ever public investment in science for poverty alleviation) (DFID, 2005). Already small, public research, university and training budgets in less-developed countries have been contracting almost uniformly, pinned back by the legacy of structural adjustment and economic underperformance. The cumulative gross domestic expenditure on research in the 44 countries in sub-Saharan Africa accounts for 0.5 per cent of the global total. By contrast, this is less than one third of Brazil's expenditure. Europe, Canada, the United States and Japan account for around 80 per cent of the total expenditure on public research (Pardey *et al.*, 2006).

One of the most problematic issues of this massive shift from public to private funding of research and development is that of 'market failure';[38] the market does not and indeed cannot respond to the needs of the poor. And as the United Nations Development Programme (2001: 3) articulates it: 'Technology is created in response to market pressures – not the needs of poor people, who have little purchasing power.' Thus we can talk of 'technological', 'digital' and 'molecular' divides in a very real sense. Perhaps the most compelling and important such divide is the '10/90 Gap' where 90 per cent of all medical research is targeted at only 10 per cent of the world's population (GFHR, 1999). This enormous inequality is exacerbated when one considers the very real differences in health profiles between rich and poor: the types of illnesses suffered by people in developed countries (lifestyle-related illnesses and cancer) and developing ones (infectious diseases) are so completely different that there is little opportunity even for the trickle-down of medicines developed in and for the West. There is simply very little incentive for the private sector to develop vaccines for HIV, malaria or tuberculosis. This is particularly problematic for HIV – as different strains (or clades) of the virus are region-specific, there is virtually no demand articulated through the market for clades that rarely occur in Europe and North America. Suturing the private sector to markets with no purchasing power in order to produce complex, risky technologies means thinking about innovation on a grand scale, and thinking very creatively about the sorts of institutional arrangements, organizational forms and funding streams that can work in those contexts.

An additional layer of complexity is related to changes in the way research is taking place. Research is becoming increasingly complex. Biotechnology, and potentially nanotechnology in the future, require increasing specialization, sophistication and resources (Orsenigo *et al.*, 1999). For example, the estimated average cost of developing a drug and taking it to market was around $400 million in 2000; only a small proportion of drugs make it to the marketplace, and it may take decades for this to happen. The potential costs involved mean that research is becoming increasingly risky profit-making enterprise (DiMasi *et al.*, 2003). The frontiers of research and development are moving forward ever faster, and increasing reliance on so-called 'platform technologies' means that promoting biotechnologies, for example, is increasingly reliant on certain levels of ICT capability (bioinformatics for example). This means fewer and fewer organizations are able to undertake all tasks in complex research. As technological innovation diverges in new, sometimes quite unexpected, directions it becomes more and more difficult to maintain expertise and capacity in many different fields, and specialization of function is becoming the norm within organizations. It is not difficult to understand why new organizational forms are emerging to deal with research and development, especially in relation to the needs of the world's developing countries.

New organizational forms: global public health partnerships

Combating HIV in clearly a priority, and one area in which science and technology, allied with appropriate public health measures, could make a major difference in developing countries. The International Aids Vaccine Initiative (IAVI) was founded in 1996 to assist in researching and developing vaccine candidates, develop policy, and serve as an advocate of HIV vaccine research around the world, with the goal of ensuring that any viable vaccine is affordable in the countries where it is most needed. IAVI functions as a public–private partnership, fusing together elements of the public and private sectors in a complementary way. IAVI is high-profile, but its levels of funding continue to be dwarfed by organizations such as the US National Institute of Health (although by 2004 IAVI had raised around $340 million). It has, however, been successful in securing funding from private foundations (such as the Rockefeller and Bill and Melinda Gates Foundations) and multilateral or bilateral donors. IAVI operates in 22 countries and seeks to engage with the public and private sectors in developed countries and with research organizations in developing countries. The main thrust of IAVI's work is through what it terms 'product development partnerships', working with partners to develop candidate vaccines – mainly in sub-Saharan Africa and India – that are specific for the variations of HIV that dominate in those regions. IAVI acts as a sort of venture capital-ist, investigating and investing in promising candidate vaccines which, although technologically exciting, would not be taken forward by the private sector alone. IAVI maintains a portfolio of the candidate vaccines it supports, choosing to spread its invest-ments widely in order to maintain the best overall chances of success (Chataway and Smith, 2006). It funds projects at the developmental, vaccine trial stage, rather than the 'upstream' stage as government research councils might, and in doing so seeks to provide private sector support where otherwise there would be none. Besides funding candidate vaccines (mainly developed in the private sector) through preliminary and possibly follow-up field trials, IAVI has an extremely important advocacy role. Preparing communities for vaccine trials, identifying potential manufacturers, and ensuring that vaccines will be relatively cheap (and paid for) are all important subsidiary activities. These activities, besides their clinical and economic value, are undertaken with a view to creating a public 'demand' for a vaccine in developed and developing countries. In raising the profile of HIV vaccine research IAVI seeks to put donor support for vaccine development, and donor and developing country support for vaccine purchase and distribution, firmly on the agenda. Producing a vaccine against HIV is proving to be exceptionally difficult and several hitherto promising candidate vaccines have performed disappointingly in human trials. Nevertheless IAVI represents an innovative model for research partnerships with the decentralization of research into the countries and communities where its outcomes will have most impact. In some respects it has inverted the traditional idea of a public–private partnership: the publicly funded body, IAVI, is providing the capital and market incentives for the private sector to take vaccine development further than it might otherwise. The momentum and policy debate IAVI creates means that if a successful vaccine were to be developed there would be funding and an infrastructure to ensure those most in need receive it.[39]

IAVI represents a new model for organizing technological research for development. Since the 1990s there has been an explosion in the number of public–private partnerships involved in developing technologies as global public goods applicable primarily in developing countries. Initiatives similar to IAVI have formed for malaria (Roll Back Malaria for example) and tuberculosis (Stop TB Partnership). Some are concerned with 'high science' such as vaccine development and some with much simpler technologies such as the provision of insecticide-impregnated bednets to limit exposure to mosquitoes (the Malaria Partnership). In veterinary science, the East Coast Fever Vaccine Project, based at the International Livestock Research Institute, has been a complex partnership between public and private sector organizations in three continents; it represents one of the most sophisticated examples of the CGIAR developing public–private partnerships – even if their efforts to develop a vaccine for East Coast Fever are also struggling to make the necessary technological breakthrough (Smith, 2005). Also in agriculture, the *Striga* Control Project, coordinated by the African Agricultural Technology Foundation, aims to develop *striga*-resistant maize through partnerships between public sector organizations from the CGIAR and the Kenyan Agricultural Research Institute and private sector organizations including Monsanto and Syngenta. This project released its first resistant maize in 2005 and now several Kenyan seed companies are marketing the product (Manyong *et al.*, 2007). Public–private partnerships such as these are based on the growing recognition that the actions of one sector or organization can reverberate for others – and may produce 'win–win' situations in 'modifying' the market to promote the development of suitable technologies. There are uncertainties, however, including the differing ethical standpoints and priorities of different partners,[40] difficulties in managing the international aspects of complex collaborations, and the not-to-be-underestimated complexity of the science (Buse and Walt, 2000). Well-managed public–private partnerships nevertheless seem to represent a way to organize research that overcomes some of the problems associated with institutionalized public sector-led research or market-led private sector research.

Intellectual property rights and other incentives

There is some debate regarding the value of intellectual property rights (IPR) for less-developed countries. Intellectual property rights are meant to ensure temporary commercial rights through patents so that innovators can gain benefit for their efforts. IPR in theory are designed to stimulate private sector innovation, encourage the use of new innovations in productive activity (whereby innovators gain reward for their work), the dissemination of new knowledge (providing a legal basis for licensing, procurement, et cetera), and the stimulation of innovation by other enterprises (patents providing a source of information for spin-off innovation) (Lall, 2001). The system is meant to encourage innovation and economic growth, and diversification and specialization in upstream discovery and downstream commercialization. The system is problematic for developing countries, however, and the strengthening of intellectual property regulations through TRIPS (trade-related aspects of intellectual property rights) has probably not helped (World Bank, 2001). Societal and economic benefits derived through intellectual property are dependent on the nature of a country's economy and the nature of technological activity. Essentially the significance of the IPR concept is related to levels of economic development; the main beneficiaries of TRIPS are the advanced countries that produce innovations (Lall, 2001). There are relatively few benefits in terms of stimulating local innovation in developing countries, as technological activity in such countries tends to focus on learning to use imported technologies rather than to innovate new technologies. In this context weak IPR could assist local firms to build technological capabilities.[41] Evidence suggests that strong IPR only begin to benefit countries with *per capita* incomes above $7,750, as they move away from building local capabilities through copying and begin to engage in more innovative activities.

Indeed, countries with lower *per capita* incomes may find the costs outweigh any benefits – IPR protection raises costs for imported products and new technologies, and curtails opportunities for local firms who might otherwise engage in imitative activities (Maskus, 2000). IPR remain an issue, driving some types of innovation while constraining others. Intellectual property rights are problematic, raising the costs of vital technologies in developing countries and playing a role in discouraging the development of technologies like country-specific vaccines.[42]

Organizations such as IAVI seek ways to circumvent this, promoting differential intellectual property arrangements that allow the private sector companies it supports to price freely in developed country markets but obliging them to price affordably in developing country markets, should they develop a successful vaccine. Indeed, the development of mechanisms and incentives to short-circuit the impacts of IPR and the inability of markets to articulate demand are evolving rapidly. Advance purchase arrangements, where donors and other agencies commit to purchasing health innovations as they are developed, may provide another powerful tool to overcome the skewed nature of markets and intellectual property, and stimulate demand. The idea of mechanisms to 'pull' research towards developmental goals has been taken up by several influential organizations, including bilateral donors and the Global Fund to Fight AIDS, Tuberculosis and Malaria (Kremer and Glennerster, 2004).

Of course, once innovations are finally off-patent it is easy to discern the impact of technology on development in terms of both the cheaper provision of drugs and economic growth in countries capable of reverse engineering and manufacturing pharmaceutical products – and this perhaps underlines exactly why we need to think about IPR and markets in a more holistic and developmental way. Indian pharmaceutical companies such as Dr Reddy's and Ranbaxy have become global players on the back of successful reverse engineering and manufacture of generic drugs (Chataway *et al.*, 2007). Building technological capabilities in this way is allowing the larger Indian pharmaceuticals to build a platform for future expansion, and this growth is already beginning to shift the balance of power in the global industry (Simonetti *et al.*, 2007).

Conclusion

This chapter has explored new ways in which technology can be more made appropriate, and more accessible, for people in developing countries. Thinking about knowledge and how it is valued in a broader, contextualized way – and trying to understand how it flows and is used innovatively – provides us with a conceptual framework to think about how technologies are developed, adapted and disseminated that is far more nuanced than ideas of simple 'technology transfer'. Understanding that the value of knowledge lies primarily in its context and contingency assists us in moving away from unhelpful and arbitrary distinctions between 'scientific' and 'indigenous' knowledge. Knowledge ought not to be valued for its subjective appeal, but inherently and contextually in its application and relevance. Understanding how knowledge interrelates and is learnt is also important. Framing these interactions as a complex system of feedback, as opposed to a linear pathway, places due emphasis on interaction and learning as key developmental processes in the act of innovation and advancement of appropriate and effective technological interventions. Innovation involves 'the use of new ideas, new technologies or new ways of doing things in a place or by people where they have not been used before' (Barnett, 2004: 1): learning, interaction and the application and accumulation of knowledge in new contexts and in new ways are vital. Placing knowledge at the centre of 'making technology work for the poor' explains the question mark in this chapter's title. Making technologies work for the poor is not about the fabrication of technologies themselves; as the case of IDE and the treadle pump shows, it is about enabling people to make technology work for them through learning, capacity building and enabling policy.

Thinking about technological innovation also demands an emphasis on markets. We can think about markets in two inter-related ways with regard to technology for development. First, we can think about ways technologies may aid the workings of markets, and, on a smaller scale, that does indeed seem to be the case. The impact of technologies in effecting big shifts in the ability of those in developing countries to compete more effec-tively globally seems limited thus far, however. Second, and importantly, we need to think hard about the role markets play in promoting research and development aimed at solving problems that are most prevalent in less-developed countries. The 'digital divide', 'molecular divide', and most importantly the '10/90 gap' illustrate the enormous disconnect between provision and need that the market is unable to articulate, as developing countries simply do not have the weight of resources to push research, development and innovation in the directions they needs to travel.

As public sector funding for science and technological develop-ment dwindles and is dwarfed by the private sector, we need to think hard about how we can develop organizations, institutions and instruments to articulate demand and mobilize the private sector. There are examples of new organizational formations in agriculture and in health, but perhaps the highest profile – if not yet successful in terms of drug development – has been the International Aids Vaccine Initiative. New relationships between the public and private sector are likely to become even more important in the future; indeed, we are already reformulating what we mean by 'public' and 'private', and, as the science becomes more specialized, we will need to work hard to develop mechanisms to govern increasingly complex relationships and increasingly complex science. That will be the focus of the next chapter.

Further reading

Chambers, R. (1993) *Challenging the Professions: Frontiers for Rural Development,* Intermediate Technology Publications, London.

Forbes, N. and D. Wield (2002) *From Followers to Leaders: Managing Technology and Innovation,* Routledge, London.

Kremer, M. and R. Glennerster (2004) *Strong Medicine: Creating Incentives for Pharmaceutical Research on Neglected Diseases,* Princeton University Press, Princeton NJ.

Richards, P. (1985) *Indigenous Agricultural Revolution,* Methuen, London.

Schumacher, E.F. (1973) *Small is Beautiful: Economics As If People Mattered,* Hartley and Marks, London.

4 | Governing Technologies for Development

As the previous chapters have illustrated, the relationships between science and society, and technology and development, are extremely complex. The frontiers of technological development are rapidly advancing, new organizational arrangements are producing technologies in ever more non-linear ways, and poverty and underdevelopment remain as intractable as ever. This context throws questions about how we should govern technology for development into sharp relief. Globalization is rapidly connecting the different scales at which our lives are lived: seeds planted in a farmer's field may have been bred and developed a continent away; collaborations link together the public and private; governments and NGOs relate in new, and old, ways; knowledge ebbs and flows; and powerful, prevailing and countervailing scientific and developmental discourses shape agendas, impact upon policies and subtly shift values and angles of debate. As science changes into a transnational, collaborative undertaking, and the technologies produced – for example, biotechnologies, biofuels and nanotechnologies – transcend national boundaries and potentially impact on all of us, governance becomes less about the role of governments and more about governing systems and networks (Lyall and Tait, 2005). States are less and less able to deal with the production of new technologies and their consequences, and science and new technologies can serve to drive new methods of decision making, new models of representation and new modes of governance.

All technologies carry with them risks, be they foreseen, unforeseen or little understood. Conversely, the benefits of technologies may be far greater than we can foresee. We respond to these uncertainties by attempting to maximize the benefits and minimize the risks of technological change. Doing so is not easy. Technologies are so completely bound up in everything we do that it is virtually impossible to separate out science from society; and new technologies spread and are taken up at an accelerating rate, often in the slipstream or eddies of existing technologies. DDT was first seen as a saviour and later became a pariah. The Green Revolution doubled cereal yields but it had adverse impacts on livelihoods and the environment. Genetically modified plants are suspected in some quarters of any number of environmental impacts, and there is a real feeling that once they are planted we cannot change our minds and undo their influence. Human cloning, the promotion of biofuels, childhood vaccinations – all raise ethical and practical dilemmas regarding our relationship to science and technology. Governance needs to be reflexive, conceptually broad and ideally as agreeable to as many interest groups and members of society as possible. The concept of 'risk', what it means and to whom, becomes central to any debate about the governance of technology.

Governance, mainly 'good' versus 'bad' governance, has been a central debate within development as well. Over the past fifty years the delineations of the state in developing countries have been shifted and eroded constantly by colonial rule, then decolonization, the influence of the World Bank and IMF, relationships with donors and, depressingly regularly, limited democracy and state capacity. The context in which we must develop mechanisms to govern the potential and threat of new technologies is complex and multi-layered: long-held dichotomies are being broken down, the technological frontier is advancing ever faster, and new technologies – perhaps some we cannot yet imagine –

will challenge our vision, our ethics and our societies to adapt and evolve. This chapter aims to highlight some of the ideas that shape our thinking regarding the governance of technology, and to highlight how various aspects of governance manifest themselves in the contexts of developing countries.

Biofuels: 'a crime against humanity?'

When the price of oil rose to an all-time high, concerns were raised about alternative fuels, and as we became increasingly concerned about climate change, biofuels (and more specifically liquid biofuel and fossil fuel blends) began to seem like a possible solution. The United States, the European Union, Brazil and a few other countries are actively supporting the production of liquid biofuels from agriculture, usually maize or sugar cane for ethanol, and various oil crops for biodiesel. Other developing countries, including India and East African countries, are planting and exploring opportunities for oil crops such as *jatropha curca*. On the face of it biofuels promise numerous social, economic and environmental benefits, mitigating against climate change, generating rural employment and contributing to energy security. Brazil has an active and well-developed bioenergy sector producing ethanol from sugar cane, and several foundations in India and East Africa, such as the Vanilla Foundation and Jatropha Foundation, are promoting the development of large oil seed plantations.

Alongside this, rising food prices have forced approximately 100 million more people into poverty, according to the World Bank (2008) (see box). Meanwhile the United States and Europe have planned to increase progressively the portion of biofuels that are blended into petrol. The promise and risks of biofuel production highlight the confluence between technologies and

The cost of oil: the price of food?

Not only oil prices are rising. Food prices increased 140 per cent from January 2002 to February 2008 and staples such as grains and oil seeds doubled in price in just a year. Several reasons have been cited, including rising oil prices, the weakening US dollar, droughts, speculators and increasing demand for food in developing countries. Biofuels have been cited as another factor, although according to some sources a minor one. In May 2008 the US Secretary of Agriculture claimed analysis showed that biofuel production contributed only 2–3 per cent to increases in food prices.[43] However, in July 2008 a leaked World Bank document calculated that biofuel production was responsible for 75 per cent of the increase in food prices between 2002 and 2008. Increased biofuel production led to increased demand for food crops, leading in turn to large-scale land-use changes which reduced supplies of crops such as wheat that compete with food crops used for biofuels (Mitchell, 2008).

globalization. The United Nations' independent expert on the right to food has cited biofuels as a 'crime against humanity' and called for a five-year moratorium on further biofuel production.[44] Several European Union countries have expressed a need for a more cautious approach.

The United States has so far not issued a statement to the effect that it will reconsider biofuel production. Biofuel production allows farmers and industry to develop new markets, and the United States and European Union support this development through the subsidization of biofuels. These measures include issuing mandates that create demand for uneconomic biofuels, tariffs which protect domestic industries by limiting imports of cheaper biofuels, and subsidies along the entire biofuel value chain

(Oxfam, 2008). According to Oxfam, biofuel policy, ostensibly designed to support the development of a sustainable energy supply that ought to benefit developed and developing countries alike, feeds rather more obviously into developed countries' interests.

There are issues with the science too. Much of the original attraction of biofuels lay in their perceived greenhouse gas neutrality. The argument goes that as crops grow they fix carbon from the atmosphere. When they are burned as biofuel this carbon is simply released back, so that, over the life cycle of the fuel, the net impact on atmospheric carbon is neutral. In reality, of course, there are emissions associated with all stages of the life cycle of biofuels – for example, the use of nitrogen-based fertilizers and machinery, the refining process, and the export–import transportation of biofuels. In practice, biofuels do not have to be carbon-neutral, they only need to emit less carbon than the equivalent fossil fuels if they are to have a beneficial impact.[45] However, any greenhouse gas saving needs to be offset against opportunity cost, land-use changes and rises in food prices if we are to understand whether they ought to be pursued or not.

Biofuels present a complicated issue. Their production in North America and Europe is heavily influencing food prices. They may be produced more sustainably in developing countries. Brazil has pursued production of sugar cane ethanol since the threat of oil crises in the 1970s and possesses an efficient system of harvesting, processing and the burning of waste to fuel the process itself. Despite this, in 2007 Brazil only managed to provide for 3 per cent of its energy needs through biofuel production (De Almeida *et al.*, 2007). Biofuel production may present opportunities in other developing countries; oil seed production of crops like *jatropha curca* has been promoted in India and Africa. *Jatropha* can grow on wasteland unsuitable for crop production and in India its production is incentivized as part of

India's long-term strategy to become energy self-sufficient. There is an environmental risk in monocropping oil seed – and if it does prove lucrative to farmers, they may choose to grow it on crop-bearing land, consequently threatening food production in new ways. Ghana and Uganda have recently rejected the widespread introduction of *jatropha*, claiming they cannot sustain production and that pristine environments remain one of their primary resources. Similar arguments have been raised over palm oil production in South East Asia, which has been blamed for the destruction of forest and biodiversity (GRAIN, 2007).

Debates surrounding highly complex technologies and their social, economic and environmental interactions are rapidly beginning to polarize, much as those around genetically modified crops did in the 1990s. On the one hand, activists and politicians state that biofuels may be a crime against humanity and 'already we know that biofuel is worse for the planet than petroleum'.[46] In response, Brazilian President Lula da Silva has commented thus:

> Certain myths about biofuels must be put to rest. Ethanol use does not threaten the environment. Neither does sugar cane cause damage to rainforests. . . . Sugar cane does, however, help to recover degraded pasture lands . . . which can then be brought back into agricultural use.[47]

It is difficult to unpick interests and values from scientific 'facts', and when we are trying to analyse such complex issues there may be no such things as 'facts'. Biofuel production, its current and future impacts and potential, will be shaped by interests and decision makers at multiple levels and across many contexts. 'Risk' and benefits may be expressed and lived in many ways from different perspectives. The current biofuel debate highlights many of the difficulties of governing technology; one of the primary difficulties revolves around what we even mean by risk in this context.

Risk and regulation

One of the most important ideas regarding risk is that society's concerns have fundamentally shifted from the production and distribution of goods to the regulation and allocation of 'bads', such as pollution, or the impacts of climate change (Beck, 1992). There has been a discernible shift towards the 'taming of risk' (Yearley, 2005: 130), in the sense that our understanding of risk and probability has improved, and that certain forms of exposure to risk have been reduced. Modernist thought suggested that progress and control of nature meant risks were diminishing – disease could be controlled and food supply secured through better farm management and the application of science, for example. However, this positive perspective on science and the management of risk has been moderated by changes in the nature of twentieth-century technologies: modern technologies are associated with new forms of risk, that may affect entire ecosystems, or even the world. Progress can lead to both novel hazards and more security (Giddens, 2002).

To an extent we have exchanged uncontrollable risks in the natural world for risky technologies whose safety depends on how they are designed and operated. Developed countries, at least, may be relatively free from dependence on the vagaries of the weather (or able to pass on the risks elsewhere – through trade in agricultural produce for example), but countries are now dependent for their security on the developers and the operators of technology, and on the institutions that regulate them. Thus, it is the regulators of risky technologies as much as the risks of nature that are to be feared. In addition, regulators of risk have elaborated increasingly sophisticated arguments, instruments and protocols to manage risk, and this has served to highlight more vividly the idea of the risks themselves. Ultimately, given that no complex system can be guaranteed to be safe, regulation of risk boils down to the creation of policies and instruments that legislate for the public's exposure to risk. Here the central question becomes: how safe is safe enough? Regardless of the use of statistics and probabilities, answers to this question are inevitably subjective (Jasanoff, 1999). First, it is often impossible to calculate risk accurately. It may be possible to assess the likelihood of, say, a car crashing on any given journey, but assessing the long-term environmental risks of genetically modified crops or the implications of climate change for coastal towns is far more difficult and fraught. Uganda, for example, is often invoked as one of the African countries in which we know most about the prevalence, spread and apparent decline of HIV. However, we can class much of what we know as hearsay rather than scientific fact, although this knowledge is often represented as fact via statistics and models. Consequently, what we think we know about HIV in Uganda, and by extension how we develop appropriate policy and model risk, may not reflect the reality (Allen, 2006). Uncertainties such as the impacts of genetically modified crops or climate change may be turned into quantifiable risks as we gain more knowledge; new knowledge might allow us to produce more finely resolved models of climate change interactions that dramatically alter our understanding of climate impacts on ecosystems, for example. The risk in modelling risk is that there is always new knowledge and new insights waiting to be uncovered that may fundamentally change our understanding of process, and thus risk. Our assessment of risk is itself at risk. 'Ignorance', or not including what we do not or cannot yet know, is effectively hardwired into any risk assessment we might make. Furthermore, there are uncertainties on which we ultimately cannot legislate; risk analyses of systems with a significant human component are fundamentally dependent on how people behave (Wynne, 1992).

Second, we perceive risk in different ways. 'Expert' and 'public' understandings of risk are inevitably different (and have

Whose risk? The oral polio vaccine in northern Nigeria

When the oral polio vaccine was rejected as allegedly containing anti-fertility agents by several northern Nigerian states in 2003, concerns centred on the motivations of global polio eradication campaigns, amidst what was perceived as anti-Islamist sentiment. The boycott was spearheaded by Muslim leaders who claimed that polio vaccine contamination was a plot by Western governments to reduce Islamic populations, and segued with post-9/11 tensions as well as tensions in Nigeria between the Islamic-controlled northern states and the perception of a Christian-dominated federal government (Yahya, 2007).

often been couched in terms of the public's misunderstanding of risk, as we shall see). To take another example, debates around the introduction of genetically modified crops often revolve as much around the politics of transnational companies impinging on the rights of developing countries and their citizens to make their own decisions as around the risks and impacts of the technologies themselves (Clark *et al.*, 2007a). Similarly, debate may centre on whether food aid is acting as a means to promote genetically modified crops in southern Africa (Zerbe, 2004). Public perceptions of the experts, and vice versa, become an important component of debate on risk. Experts, when pressed, tend to make statistical claims that are often unwarranted, and public audiences are becoming particularly sensitive to the role of expertise in decision making; this scepticism becomes an important element of any decision concerned publics make regarding a risk. Furthermore, the public may be far more insightful than experts in relation to matters concerned with risk that are not strictly scientific or technical (Wynne, 1992). A typical response of experts to some of these problematic issues of risk perception is to demand 'more and better' science or public education, even though additional insight is seldom gained from these approaches (Yearley, 2005).

Risk is embedded not only in the ways in which society interacts with technologies and the production of knowledge and expertise, but also in the capacity of countries to regulate and manage the process that interrelates expertise, interests, and analyses of the allocation of benefits and risk. This is problematic in developing countries for two reasons. First, developing countries tend to be more vulnerable to certain major risks, their publics to be more exposed and less well-equipped to deal with risks, and their governments to be similarly ill-equipped. This is true for any number of potential risks – climatic, economic, and technological (Blaikie *et al.*, 1994). This vulnerability intensifies risk and amplifies its impact, and therefore perhaps places even greater emphasis on the need for effective regulation of risk. Second, developing countries are often poorly prepared to regulate risk. They lack the expertise, legal instruments or regulatory frameworks to make effective decisions. International treaties such as the Cartagena Protocol aim to provide guidance and an international context for risk regulation, but often developing countries struggle to keep pace with the advance of the technological frontier.

Biosafety and biotechnology in Kenya

Kenya is fertile ground for agricultural research and development, and has become something of a hub for agricultural biotechnological research in East Africa, with over ten years' experience of mainly public–private, partnership-driven development in this field. Kenya has been engaging with so-called 'low' biotechnologies such as tissue culture (discussed in Chapter 2) and biofertilizers for several decades (Odame *et al.*, 2003). In 1991 a partnership between the Kenyan Agricultural Research Institute, the United States Agency for International Development and Monsanto began to develop Kenya's first 'modern' biotechnology, a genetically modified virus-resistant sweet potato. The technology has received much attention as East Africa's first 'indigenous' GM crop, most recently in terms of its inability to offer protection against viruses.[48] Despite this initial failure, research is still ongoing and new varieties of sweet potato are being developed for testing. Other GM crops are in development in Kenya, again through partnerships, including virus-resistant cassava and insect-resistant maize and cotton. No crops have yet moved beyond contained trials.

Formal state instruments of governing and regulating biotechnology in Kenya have been coordinated rather loosely and developed almost in reaction to technological advances. A succession of donors have sponsored different elements in Kenya's evolving biosafety systems. The first large-scale biosafety project started in 1993, and Kenya was one of four countries chosen to develop a 'biotechnology platform' targeted at poverty alleviation. The project involved developing elements of specific technologies alongside national regulatory and biosafety capacity. This project fed into a subsequent United Nations Environment Programme project, again aimed at developing biosafety frameworks. These projects both interacted with a newly formed Council of Science and Technology that went on to produce a national biosafety framework in 1999. This framework addressed research and development, but not release of biotechnologies for commercial use.[49] The result of the interventions of these multiple donors is Kenya's current biosafety regulatory system, little adapted from the 1999 framework, which is a complicated amalgamation of five government ministries, five government departments and eight government acts (Harsh, 2005). Despite intense donor support, as of late 2007, a Kenya biosafety bill had still to be enacted by Parliament.

Kenya's complex biosafety system and tardiness in developing legislation have led to a situation in which policy is struggling to keep pace with the development of technology. Neighbouring Uganda, in contrast, has taken a position that no GM research or trials will occur until a policy and regulatory system are prepared and approved. Kenya is left to react to technology. The GM sweet potato project began in 1991, long before the formulation of biosafety guidelines in 1998; then, in the implementation stage, the import of GM sweet potato material came just a few months after the biosafety guidelines were issued – leaving critics to question just how much research agendas were driving biosafety developments (*ibid.*). The sheer complexity of the ministries, departments and acts that constitute Kenya's system means that linkages within the system and with other actors are weak; consequently, there is little opportunity to learn and to refine policy and systems. Currently, Kenya's regulatory system allows it to approve technologies, but does not include mechanisms to enforce regulation or systems for strategic decision making regarding future technology development. As regulations cannot be enforced through the courts, there is no accountability for decisions. The private sector, and Kenya's many international donors and international research institutes, cannot be held accountable for the adverse effects of their actions on public and farmers, should they violate biosafety guidelines. Kenya's lack of legal authority and capacity to regulate technology is by no means unique and underlines why, especially in the context of developing countries, we need to take a more panoptic view of risk and regulation than that traditionally offered by 'government'.

The ungovernable rise of governance

The concept of governance emerged in the 1990s through a series of debates regarding the role of the state in modern society (Jordan *et al.*, 2005; World Bank, 1994). This debate was rooted in the realization that governments were no longer able to cope with problems or deal with demands that are too numerous and too contradictory (Stoker, 1998). With regard to developing countries, the debate also revolved around the capacity of the state to govern effectively. The logical conclusion is that the developing country state must share its power with non-political agents, forming partnerships and networks with the private sector, donors, NGOs and other civil society groups. There is a clear shift from command and control regulatory instruments towards more informal processes through which non-political actors are gradually allowed to coordinate and organize themselves. This process supposedly marks a shift from 'hierarchy' to 'heterarchy', from the institutional order of domestically controlled markets and state strength towards self-organizing networks and organizational coordination (Jessop, 1998). We can conceive of governance as a set of networks and social interactions rather than a political process of government institutions (Pierre and Peters, 2000). Despite enthusiasm for this society-centric conceptualization of governance, in reality heterarchy fails to serve society as a whole. Instead, it serves the fragmented and contradictory interests of particular social groups and individuals, promoting their specific conceptions of the 'common good'.

From governments to governance

In this context we can begin to understand the processes that lead to the dichotomization of debates surrounding particular technologies. Agricultural biotechnology is perhaps the most telling example of this: the debate surrounding the appropriateness of GM crops for developing countries has become increasingly divisive and divided. At one end of the spectrum, international NGOs like Action Aid or Greenpeace argue there are no environmental or economic benefits, only risks, to be gained from agricultural biotechnologies in their current form (Action Aid, 2003). At the other end of the spectrum, scientists like Dr Florence Wambugu of Africa Harvest make bold claims: 'In Africa GM food could almost literally weed out poverty' (*New Scientist*, 2004). Tellingly, and perhaps an indication that the notion of governance is taking root, some of the most diverse opinions come from developing countries. Florence Wambugu is a Kenyan, and often uses this fact as a rhetorical device to show that she knows better than Greenpeace or Oxfam what poor African farmers need (Wambugu, 2001). Possibly the most powerful counter-arguments come from Vandana Shiva, an Indian (cf. Shiva, 1993). These may be Southern voices but their concerns reflect on global issues and represent global interests, and herein lies a problem of governance. Wambugu represents – or at least is accused of representing, which means virtually the same thing in the context of this debate – the interests of multinational companies such as Monsanto and, avowedly, pro-biotechnology donors such as USAID (cf. Harsh, 2005). Shiva is taken to be a traditional, anti-capitalist, anti-globalization activist. In the same way that Greenpeace or Action Aid, or Monsanto for that matter, cannot claim to represent the authentic views of resource-poor farmers, activists from their own social *milieus* and with their own intellectual agendas are always in some way disconnected from the decision-making processes and needs of the people whom they claim to represent (cf. Fowler, 2000). This material distance becomes a rhetorical device in itself. One of the most prominent scientists associated with the Green Revolution,

Norman Borlaug, stated in an interview 'some of the environmental lobbyists of the Western nations are the salt of the earth but many of them are elitists. They've never experienced the physical sensation of hunger. They do their lobbying from comfortable office suites in Washington or Brussels.'[50] Similar sentiments were expressed by Tony Hall, the US Ambassador to the World Food Programme, regarding Zambia's decision to reject GM food aid in 2002. He accused 'well-fed' European experts of endangering the lives of millions of Africans out of sheer ignorance.[51] The issue of GM food aid and the Southern African famine of 2002 did seem to be a case of one well-fed Western politician arguing with another.

GM food aid and Zambia: heterarchical governance?

By early 2002, Southern Africa was facing the worst food crisis in a decade, as some sixteen million people faced serious food shortages due to a complex combination of factors including relatively insignificant climate shocks, HIV, debt, political problems in Zimbabwe and the collapse of commercial maize production (Vogel and Smith, 2002). In October 2002, the governments of Malawi,[52] Mozambique, Zambia and Zimbabwe made the decision to reject the importation of US food aid amid concerns over the inclusion of genetically modified maize. The United States offered aid in kind and could not guarantee that its maize did not contain GM maize, whereas most European donors offered cash to purchase maize on the open market. This decision quickly meant that Southern Africa was incorporated into existing trans-Atlantic debates over trade in GMOs.[53] Pro- and anti-GM lobbies sought to use the crisis to articulate their positions over agricultural biotechnology, genetically modified crops, trade, and their roles in development. In 2002, very few Southern African countries had established their own national biosafety protocols or ratified the Cartagena Protocol, meaning they had very little recourse to any legal apparatus when deciding how to deal with food aid. GM food aid was rejected by the four countries on two fronts: first, and most tenuously, the possible risk to human health in consuming the maize; and, second, the possible impacts on future exportation of organic and non-GM maize if inadvertent cross-fertilization was to occur.

GM maize referred to Bt maize, which was maize that had been genetically modified to express the bacterial *Bacillus thuringiensis* toxin, which is poisonous to insect pests. This was achieved by inserting a gene from the Bt pathogen microorganism into the maize genome. The Bt microorganism has also been inserted into other crops such as cotton with the aim of increasing insect pest resistance. Bt maize is widely grown across the United States, although debate still ensues regarding its efficacy and impacts, particularly in developing countries.[54]

Malawi, Mozambique and Zimbabwe eventually accepted food aid on the proviso that all maize was milled prior to importation to avoid contamination.[55] Zambia, however, continued to refuse to accept imports. Within Zambia there had been consultation regarding the issue: church groups, NGOs and farmers' groups were consulted,[56] and independent scientific advice was sought. A team of government scientists was commissioned and spent time in laboratories in the US, the UK, Norway and the headquarters of the European Union. The issue was highly political within Zambia. Opposition groups were very vocal in their criticism of the President, Levy Mwanawasa, who in turn stuck to his position. The President's position can be explained partly by the fact that he did not enjoy broad support at home, and aligning with a range of civil society actors, and being seen to display his authority in the face of international pressure, was good for his prestige (Smith, 2003). The position of the scientific committee can be explained partly by the fact that Zambia does not have any significant technology-led private sector, so scientists were perhaps more able to be critical than might have been the case in South Africa or Kenya, where private-sector or donor funding plays such a key role in research.

More significantly, Zambia's decision became the nexus for ferocious international debate. Andrew Natsios, head of USAID, contended that anti-GM groups were 'putting millions of lives at risk in a most despicable way' (cited in Vidal, 2002). Ann Veneman, the United States Secretary of Agriculture, said of the actions of groups like Greenpeace that 'instead of helping hungry people, these individuals and organizations are embarking on an irresponsible campaign to spread misinformation and create an atmosphere of fear'.[57] The anti-GM lobby countered by arguing that the US approach was simply a way to gain positive public relations for agricultural biotechnologies and introduce GM maize into Southern African countries while the recipients had little choice, thus opening them to the introduction of GM crops in the future. In any case, both Malawi and Zambia claimed they could source sufficient food within the region. S. K. Mubukwanu, the Zambian High Commissioner in London, stated that 'we can get more than 200,000 tonnes from South Africa. . . . All we need is help with the logistics' (cited in Vidal, 2002).

Outside of the region the issue caused tensions between the United States and the European Union to escalate. In January 2003, Paul Nielsen, the EU's Overseas Aid Chief, accused Robert Zoellnick of lying when the US Trade Representative stated that EU governments had threatened to withdraw aid from developing countries that used GMOs. He continued:

This is a strange discussion. Very strange, we are approaching a point where I would be tempted to say I would be proposing a deal to the Americans which would create a more normal situation. The deal would be this: if the Americans would stop lying about us, we would stop telling the truth about them. This is a proposal for normalizing the discussion.[58]

Europe's position would ultimately provide justification for the United States filing a case with the World Trade Organization regarding Europe's moratorium on importing GMOs. Zoellnick (2003) argued that 'this dangerous effect of the EU's moratorium became painfully evident last fall when some famine-stricken African countries refused US food aid because of fabricated fears stoked by irresponsible rhetoric about food safety'.

The case of GM food aid in Southern Africa does little to bolster the idea that heterarchy as a concept means much in developing countries (see box on p. 106). Debates regarding the consumption of GM maize in the midst of potential famine were played out in offices and meeting rooms in the United States, Europe and Lusaka by 'well-fed' policy makers and lobbyists. A lack of government regulation may have created space for governance, but it did not create networks and mechanisms to include those most affected by the decision.

The idea of 'governance' highlights the changing nature of the policy process that has occurred over the past few decades. It sensitizes us to the increasing variety and number of contexts and actors involved in the making of public policy. Thinking in terms of governance demands that we consider all the actors, locations and activities involved in the policy-making process, not simply the core apparatus of the state.

Many of the complicating factors identified in the application of the governance agenda to science and technology-related issues arise from the complex interactions between, on the one hand, the still-necessary, or desirable, government-based regulation and control, and, on the other, the core themes of the governance agenda – in particular the contrasting and occasionally incompatible requirements for policy decisions to be evidence-based and at the same time engender a greater degree of stakeholder engagement in policy making (Lyall and Tait, 2005: 179). If we are to engage in deliberative and participatory processes around issues of science and technology, thought needs to be given to mechanisms and processes that engage with the people who will engage most closely with the technology.

Mali, GM crops and citizens' juries

Towards the end of January 2006, 45 Malian farmers gathered in Sikasso to discuss the role of GM crops in the future of the country's agriculture. L'ECID (L'Espace Citoyen d'Interpellation Démocratique, or Citizens' Space for Democratic Deliberation) aimed at allowing farmers the opportunity to engage in the policy-making process by sharing knowledge and making a series of recommendations to policy makers. L'ECID represented an experiment in deliberative democracy regarding the role of new technologies in Mali's agricultural system. The deliberation process lasted for four days and was based on the model of a citizens' jury. This participatory platform draws on some of the symbolism and practice of a legal trial by jury. It gives the 'jury', the participants, the opportunity to cross-examine and question expert 'witnesses', who represent a variety of perspectives, enabling the jury to develop a summary of their conclusions. An oversight panel was appointed to ensure the rigour of the process and to try to ensure that decision makers showed commitment to the process and its findings (Bryant, 2009).

L'ECID employed a selection process to identify the 45 farmers/producers from Sikasso Region. The selection process was designed to reflect local diversity and all sectors of the population. After meeting with expert witnesses, in some cases more than once, the jury's recommendations included a unanimous rejection of GM crops and instead 'proposed a package of recommendations to strengthen traditional agricultural practice and support local farmers'.[59] It is difficult to discern the concrete impact of deliberative processes on broader policy-making processes. Nevertheless, in June 2006, when a debate in the Malian Parliament questioned the Minister of Agriculture on the use of GM crops, many felt this was as a result of the highly publicized jury process. The jury resulted in the delay of the approval of the legislation needed before GM crops can be introduced. Commenting on his frustration over his efforts to take legislation to Parliament, one senior civil servant revealed: 'The delay has been because of the jury', and 'it has had a great impact and this has caused a problem'. The coordinator of an international biosafety project verified this opinion: 'Everyone is pointing at this Citizens' Jury in Sikasso' (Clark *et al.*, 2007a: 114). The hold-up of legislative approval is significant, as without legislation it is very difficult to introduce GM crops into the country.

In mid-2006, the Sikasso Regional Assembly sent members to a follow-up workshop where they had the opportunity to discuss the original jury's decision with some of the jurors. Sikasso, as the main agricultural region in Mali and economically very significant, carries a lot of weight in national decision making. The President of the Sikasso Regional Assembly expressed reservations regarding the growing of GM crops in Mali after the workshop (Clark *et al.*, 2007). A member of a USAID-funded biosafety project revealed that USAID had planned to organize a workshop in Mali to counteract L'ECID, but felt that the atmosphere was too hostile and would hold it elsewhere: 'This was defeatist, and . . . they have won in their ignorance' (*ibid.*: 114). As noted by others, the response by many in power to citizen deliberations which propose recommendations unfavourable to them is to dismiss the approach (Wakeford and Pimbert, 2004). Many critiques of L'ECID drew on measurement and quantification in questioning the methodology of the jury, complaining that each expert witness did not present for the same length of time, nor did each have to deal with the same number of questions. Further complaints revolved around the lack of 'citations' and 'scientific evidence' (Bryant, 2009). This harks back to the essentialism of scientific knowledge discussed in earlier chapters – although the jurors' calls for more indigenous agriculture may represent essentialism of a different hue.

The Malian citizens' jury was not perfect. There are thorny issues of representation in any democratic process, and despite best intentions the make-up of the jury will never truly represent broader opinion.[60] Regardless of its conclusions, however, it did provide an opportunity for often-excluded stakeholders to take part in debate, it raised an important issue, and it forced politicians and policy makers to take note of the opinions of a small group of farmers and producers in Mali. It is important also to note that activities of this sort may not simply represent epistemic conflicts, reconciled or not, between scientific and lay knowledge, but also different ways of being, practising and relating. They represent ontological clashes too, and this may be increasingly relevant.

Dealing with complexity in the twenty-first century

It seems we have drifted from the heady days of the post-war period, when newly formed scientific institutions would provide solutions to the problems of development, to a period when the nature and authority of science are increasingly under question. Science is placed under pressure as the risks attributed to it become more complex and difficult to quantify, as the science itself becomes ever more complex and more difficult to explain in lay terms, and as new organizational forms tie the global and local together in new ways. As the scientific frontier moves forward with greater pace and science can lay claim to technologies – biotechnologies, nanotechnologies – of enormous potential, science itself enters something of a crisis. The public are distrustful of scientists and society is increasingly wary of science (Collins and Evans, 2002).

Development is going through a similar existential crisis. Very few, if any, MDGs are likely to be met by 2015. Poverty, particularly in Africa, is becoming more entrenched, global inequality is rising, the idea of 'trickle down' neoclassical economics as the mechanism to erase poverty has become passé (Stiglitz, 2002). While developed countries are committing, if not always providing, more resources to development assistance, and bilateral development is becoming more transparent and collaborative and less tied, the impact of development looks more and more insignificant in the context of uneven access to markets and the ability to trade (Oxfam, 2002).

This double movement may represent something of a crisis of representation (Redner, 1994). The twenty-first century is a time when scientific and developmental representations of the world, how it works and how it should be governed are being more widely challenged. Somewhat lazily, we could attribute this to a flash of post-modern insight, a collective realization that optimism in modernity has been misplaced.[61] Beck has argued that science becomes more and more necessary in the same moment it becomes less and less sufficient for providing a definition of truth modern society can accept (Beck, 1992: 156). It may simply be that 'science' and 'technology' within development are becoming increasingly exposed as development itself appears to rely more and more on the promise of science and technology when it is faced with its own inability to solve intractable problems. As poverty deepens in Africa and inequalities widen elsewhere, perhaps development's existential crisis means that science, with its traditional inability to articulate risk and communicate with publics, becomes a prism that refracts broader misgivings regarding the trappings of modernization: globalization, development, the power of the transnational company, the commodification of nature.

That is not to say that science is not sometimes wrong, or that technologies do not fail, or disappoint, or amplify risk and inequality. Rather, it is to acknowledge that perhaps technologies may act as artefacts that represent broader fields of ideas and systems of values that are the deeper sources of our discomfort. In the same way that in the 1960s IR8 was taken to represent the power of science to change the world, perhaps at the turn of the century GM crops are taken to represent far more than what they are; this is true for 'activists' who claim GM crops are a conduit through which companies like Monsanto can 'own' nature or scientists who assert their power to 'weed out poverty'. This representation is apparent to degrees in the cases of Mali and Zambia. As science and technology, already so entwined with society, are entwined through globalization in new, more complex ways, this crisis of representation is not likely to dampen down. Biofuels or climate change illustrate the potential for technology to connect the global and local, urban and rural, rich and poor in hitherto completely unexpected ways.

Conclusion

This chapter described some of the complexities involved in effectively governing science. 'Risk' is a complicated and contested concept that forms a hub for much debate around science and technology. As scientific advances occur with greater frequency and technologies become ever more complex, how we deal with risk and with benefits requires more complex, reflexive systems of governance. This is reflected in the shift from formal, regulated government to informal, networked governance – and the cases presented underscore that, even if we are talking about 'government' as in the case of biosafety regulation in Kenya, we are really talking about governance. Science and technological innovation often move more quickly than formal systems of decision making.

It is almost impossible to see all ends; it would have been inconceivable twenty years ago that African countries would be demanding a comeback for DDT. Biofuels were 'good' and now it seems they are officially 'bad'. And as technologies increasingly straddle boundaries, effectively removing them, we need to think about new governance mechanisms that reflect complexity. Sweet potatoes fortified with Vitamin A or 'Golden Rice' that expresses beta-carotene demand, for example, that we think about health, environmental and agricultural implications in relation to each other.

Good governance seeks to include new decision makers, communities and individuals, and ways to reflect their divergent and value-laden interests in governing science and technology need to be developed. This means thinking about how we communicate, how science interrelates with the public, and how we reconcile multiple conceptualizations of risk, science, and technology in the world. In the oppositional politics of GM crops in Mali or GM food aid in Zambia we can see that governance can move quicker than technology, making decisions before the technology is introduced (or – in the case of debates around nanotechnologies, for example – even before it exists). Debates about globalization, free trade, national sovereignty and the precautionary principle subsume any conceivable impact of consuming milled GM maize. Ultimately these debates reflect a crisis of representation where technologies denote broader processes of development and globalization by proxy. This, then, surely reflects back on the fundamental importance science and technology play, and must play, in development.

Further reading

Crewe, E. and E. Harrison (1998) *Whose Development? An Ethnography of Aid*, Zed Books, London.

Farmer, P. (2003) *Pathologies of Power: Health, Human Rights, and the New War on the Poor*, University of California Press, Berkeley CA.

Leach, M., I. Scoones and B. Wynne (2005) *Science and Citizens: Globalization and the Challenge of Engagement*, Zed Books, London.

Lyall, C. and J. Tait (2005) *New Modes of Governance: Developing an Integrated Policy Approach to Science, Technology, Risk and the Environment*, Ashgate, Aldershot.

Murphy, J. and L. Levidow (2006) *Governing the Transatlantic Conflict over Agricultural Biotechnology: Contending Coalitions, Trade Liberalisation and Standard Setting*, Routledge, London.

Pierre, J. and B. Peters (2000) *Governance, Politics and the State*, Macmillan, London.

Conclusion | Can Technology Transform Development?

Sleeping sickness and unwanted hirsutism

Sleeping sickness, or the human form of *trypanosomiasis,* places approximately sixty million people in sub-Saharan Africa at risk and leads to 300,000 new cases per year (World Health Organization, 2000). The extreme poverty of the afflicted population has created no financial incentive to develop new drug treatments and most of the drugs currently used to treat the disease were developed more than fifty years ago. Suramin and pentamidine, used to treat early-stage disease, were developed in Germany shortly after the First World War and in 1937 respectively. Late-stage disease is predominantly treated by arsenic-containing compounds, some of which date back to 1932, such as melarsoprol (Coyne, 2001). Only melarsoprol can cross the blood-brain barrier to treat late-stage sleeping sickness. The affordability, efficacy and environmental and clinical toxicity of these drugs are of increasing concern. A third of candidates do not respond to melarsoprol; one in ten will die from the treatment itself. The drug is so corrosive it must be kept in glass vials as it eats through plastic ones.

In the 1970s the synthesis of *difluoromethylornithine*, or eflornithine, as a potential anti-cancer drug that impaired cellular division, was studied as a potential treatment for sleeping sickness. By 1985, the WHO was undertaking clinical trials in partnership with the drug's manufacturer, Merrell Dow Pharmaceuticals (Bacchi *et al.*, 1980). In some late-stage patients the clinical response was so strong that eflornithine was dubbed the 'resurrection drug' (Coyne, 2001). In 1990, Merrell was granted approval for the drug, making eflornithine the first new drug treatment for sleeping sickness in more than forty years.

Treatment with the drug was expensive, however, with a fourteen-day course of treatment costing in the region of $700. This was prohibitive given the resources available in countries where *trypanosomiasis* was endemic. Subsequently, in the short-term Merrell agreed to supply the drug to WHO at cost while WHO sought a third-party manufacturer to take on production. Uganda approved the drug in 1993, although no third-party supplier had yet been identified. In 1995 Merrell, now called Aventis as a result of a merger, finding both melarsoprol and eflornithine in its portfolio of drugs, discontinued production of eflornithine as a cost-reduction measure – given the resource-intensive nature of the synthesis, it was simply not profitable. The remaining stocks of the drug were donated to Médecins Sans Frontières (MSF) in 2000. By the end of 2000 all remaining stocks were past their expiration date, and the entire stockpile was projected to last for no more than a further six months (*ibid.*).

During the late 1990s the best efforts of the WHO and MSF to find a third-party manufacturer proved fruitless until it was noted that clinical trials in sleeping sickness patients identified hair loss as a side-effect (Pepin *et al.*, 1987). In 2000 this obser-vation led to the development, under licence from Aventis, of a topical formulation of eflornithine, Vaniqa, by another drug company, Bristol-Myers Squibb, to treat unwanted facial hair in women, primarily in the North American market. This contrast in context and response, of African sleeping sickness and facial hirsutism in Western women, and the decision to produce eflornithine for the cosmetic application and not to treat a deadly disease, led to somewhat embarrassed discussions between Aventis, Bristol-Myers Squibb, the WHO and MSF to reach some sort of solution.[62] In May 2001 Aventis signed an agreement with the WHO and MSF committing $25 million over five years to produce with Bristol-Myers Squibb sufficient quantities of eflornithine for therapeutic needs, support MSF in supplying the drugs to the patient, and support research and surveillance of sleeping sickness control programmes. During the five-year period 200,000 bottles of eflornithine were produced by Aventis, donated to the WHO and distributed by MSF, saving an estimated 110,000 lives.[63] In 2006 this agreement was renewed with a further five-year commitment by Aventis to supply eflornithine and other sleeping sickness drugs. It seems now there is a viable partnership in place to ensure the supply of therapeutic drugs for sleeping sickness, and plans to ensure the sustainability of drug manufacture and supply. Nevertheless, back in 2001 a Bristol-Myers Squibb spokesman inadvertently summed up the dichotomy in the application of technology induced by inequality: 'Before Vaniqa came on the scene, there was no reason to make eflornithine at all. Now there's a reason' (cited in Rosenberg, 2006).

Can science be transformational?

The story of eflornithine strikes at the core of the relationship between science and development. No matter how tightly science and technology are entwined with development, the relationship only ever reflects a slice of all that development represents. Eflornithine highlights the context of science, and in turn science reflects back the reality of development (and underdevelopment). Eflornithine and the decisions made regarding when to produce it and for whom reflect profound global inequality, and that inequality does not seem to be something that science and technology are able to address. Inequality in relation to technology cuts in different ways. A lack of access to resources, to knowledge or to markets, or a lack of political power, all serve to limit the ability of individuals, communities and countries to exploit opportunities fully – including advancing scientific knowledge and technological opportunities – and therefore we have to be careful that science does not serve simply to exacerbate and amplify existing structural inequalities. Furthermore, inequality is also manifested as an inability to represent one's position or articulate one's needs; eflornithine represents a good example of this. Ultimately, inequality is apparent in the relationship between opportunity and articulation, or between depilatory cream and a course of treatment against debilitating and potentially fatal illness. Our ability to exploit, adapt or appropriate technologies – coupled with our ability to interact in social networks (including, if not especially, the economy) that drive technological development and change – shape and circumscribe our ability to derive benefit or absorb risk. This relationship cannot simply be reduced to a calculus of capacity, networks and benefit/risk, even if documents such as the *UN Millennium Report* tend towards this approach; rather, it reflects the topography of deep-rooted social, political and economic problems in which science exists, that delineates who has power and subsequently opportunity and who has not.

Somewhat paradoxically, while science, as the driver of economic growth, retains all its charisma as a sort of multi-sectoral silver bullet that can improve human welfare through innovation in public health, nutrition and agriculture,[64] technological innovation has tended to exacerbate inequality through time; modernization represents, indeed advocates, this tendency. This is made explicit when one considers the history of innovation and economic development, and is implicit in calls for increased investment and emphasis on science and technology for development. Some of the most pervasive and obdurate sources of inequality are embedded in and entrenched by scientific and technological systems. This book has recounted examples of the positive impacts of science in providing solutions to the problems that beset developing countries – the stop-start development of eflornithine being a case in point – but these innovations do not necessarily translate into the sort of long-term economic development that will narrow inequalities between and within countries. Where science and technology have been cited as agents of such change, as in the case of the Asian Tigers, it can be shown to be only one, albeit important, component in complex political and economic configurations that have driven change (Castells, 1998).

Science promises something radical in its perpetual promise of Lévi-Straussian 'transformative breakthroughs' (Lévi-Strauss, 1966), but in reality represents something profoundly conservative. By its nature, science isolates problems, and a motif of this book has been the exploration of ways to overcome this tension between the tendency of science to focus on the microscopic or molecular and the need to affect macroscopic change for development. Advocating more science and by extension technology means we are not obliged to engage with the profound structural problems that inhibit development. For example, debates around access to international markets for agricultural products, prohibitive phytosanitary regulations, the rights and wrongs of agricultural subsidies, and the possible impacts of climate change might just be sidestepped if we can develop suitably high-yielding GM crops – and hence that becomes the focus of donors and decision makers. Technology may absolve us of the unlevel playing field, and in doing so allow us to turn our eyes away from the history of inequality and deep-rooted poverty that is part of our world towards a future where the black boxes of technology and development will have solved these and other problems. This Cornucopian perspective of course simplifies our relationship with technology to make a point, but – in its visions of transformation, the promises of *ex ante* studies, and the adoption of a sort of inverted Murphy's Law where everything that can go right for a technology does (Tim Searchinger, quoted in Oxfam, 2008: 6) – looks to the future and not the past. But more often than not it is in the past that we find the roots of problems that we seek to overcome.

We have to ask ourselves whether we look towards the transformational potential of science and technology simply because we do not know how to make development work. Or, perhaps more fundamentally, are we unwilling to make the concessions and sacrifices to effect the changes we need to make in order to address widening global inequalities? Certainly our collective inability to confront climate change would suggest the latter. Ultimately, in thinking about science and technology as agents to transform development, we are obliged to consider just what we mean by 'development'. If 'development' is simply making an array of interventions in problematic areas of people's lives – dealing better with illness, hunger, access to information and so on – science and technology play a fundamental role. If by 'development' we mean increasing economic growth to lift individual incomes, science, through technology, plays a role – but a role that seems increasingly less important the poorer a country is. If 'development' means to equalize inequality it seems that technology, and specifically access to technology, may hinder that process. Science, and its relationship to development, force us to interrogate what we mean and how we want the world to change, and for this reason technology, through its visibility, becomes a focal point for debate regarding development. Development by its very nature means to generate a series of confrontations. Governing technology for development is proving very thorny.

Technology as emancipation

In 1948, President Truman made his call for using the 'benefits of our scientific advances' for development (Public Papers of the Presidents of the United States, 1964: 114–15). In 1980, the Brandt Report argued that the sharing of technology is a world-wide concern and that a principal weakness of developing countries was their lack of access to technology (Brandt, 1980). Nearly a quarter of a century later, Gordon Brown expressed similar sentiments, arguing that now we had the science and technology to deal with poverty (Brown, 2004). The last sixty years have repeated a refrain of scientific breakthrough, technological promise and developmental disappointment. Rather than the progression that modernization theory promised us we have witnessed a more circular pattern of new knowledge, progress, setback and learning. This pattern, of course, much better matches the reality of scientific discovery than the one commonly portrayed (Sismondo, 2004). Science, by design or epistemology, has not engaged with the broader vistas of development. Technology, however, is increasingly understood and articulated in terms of the systems in which it has come to exist and been utilized. Hence, we are witnessing a shift towards thinking not about science and technology but, instead, about knowledge and innovation. This more critical understanding of how knowledge leads to innovation has led to the development of new models of delivering technological innovations for development. Public–private partnerships, networks of institutions, modes of organizational learning and incentives to shape demand and supply in markets all point to a more nuanced understanding of the relationship between technology and development, and indeed between science and technology. It is not clear where modernization and the blueprinting of policies, technologies and other interventions for different developing country contexts fit into this new understanding of how technological innovation can aid development. Indeed, somewhere in the matrix of learning, sharing knowledge, feedback and articulation of needs are important lessons for the grander narratives and certainties of development and modernization.

There is enormous promise in technology for development – if not the sort of transformational promise that could, in one sweep or in one moment of insight or discovery, solve the most intractable problems the world faces. Science is not *the* answer, and technology is not *the* solution; science will most likely never provide a developmental *deus ex machina*. Science and technology can be part of an answer, however, and play a central role in helping solve some of the development dilemmas and problems we face today. We must not forget, or in some cases we need to be told, that science and technology do not exist as some abstraction of a process of modernization. They are absolutely contingent on the contours of inequality and social, political and economic problems that shape our world. It is important to remind ourselves that science and technology are absolutely enmeshed in society. If we – and scientists and development practitioners and policy makers – remember that, we can begin to understand the real, integral role science and technology can play in development. To critique and question that role continually is to acknowledge its importance and place trust in the power of technology to make tangible contributions to development.

Glossary

Bioenergy is renewable energy made available from materials derived from recently alive biological sources; for example, biofuel, which is fuel derived from biological sources, or even firewood. The term may also apply to the social, economic, scientific and other technical fields associated with the utilization of biological sources for energy.

Biotechnology refers to a technological application that uses biological systems, living organisms or their derivatives to make or modify products or processes for specific applications. Biotechnology is often taken to refer to 'genetic engineering' (the direct manipulation of an organism's genes) but more accurately the term 'modern biotechnology' might be appropriate, as biotechnology can refer to processes such as the modification of plants into improved food crops through selection or hybridization.

Global public good. A true global public good should be freely available worldwide, it should be impossible to exclude people from using the good, and its use should not reduce the quantity available for others. Examples of global public goods might be the seed varieties produced during the Green Revolution. An alternative name is 'international public good'.

Green Revolution refers to the transformation of agriculture that began in Mexico, with the development of high-yielding hybrid varieties of wheat, and in the Philippines, with the development of hybrid varieties of rice. There was an associated transformation in agriculture related to how agricultural research was undertaken, agricultural extension, the use of inputs like fertilizers and technologies such as irrigation systems.

The Green Revolution raised average cereal yields but the impacts were not uniform and some critics suggest social and ecological problems were provoked.

Information and communication technology (ICT) is an umbrella term that refers to all technologies for the manipulation and communication of information. This includes for example the Internet, mobile phones, wired telephones, cameras and MP3 players.

Innovation system is a concept that stresses that the flow of technologies and information among people, institutions and enterprises is central to any innovative process. It contains the web of interactions between all the actors needed in order to turn an idea into process, product or service in a market.

Intellectual property rights are legal exclusive rights over inventions, 'creations of the mind', be they scientific, artistic or commercial. A legal patent may be granted for a new, useful and non-obvious innovation, giving the patent holder a right to prevent others from using or manufacturing the invention without a licence from the inventor for an agreed period of time.

'Platform technology' describes a technique, discipline or tool that enables a range of scientific investigations or technological applications. For example ICT, biotechnology or nanotechnology

Technological catch-up refers to the idea, derived from institutional economics, that companies or countries can, through policy and innovation, catch up with competitors or countries that would hitherto be considered technologically more advanced.

Upstream research refers to the 'basic', 'blue sky' research that must go on to make the scientific advances on which new research, technologies and innovations are built.

Notes

Introduction

1 Evenson and Gollin, 2003. The Green Revolution commonly refers to the widespread development and adoption of high-yielding varieties of staple crops that occurred in the 1960s and 1970s. Successes in yield increases were tempered by a lack of impact on poorer farmers (especially in Africa) and longer-term environmental and sometimes societal impacts.

2 Eight goals – which range from halving extreme poverty to halting the spread of HIV/AIDS and providing universal primary education, all by 2015 – that form a blueprint agreed by the world's countries and multilateral agencies.

3 The term 'platform technologies' refers to generic technologies such as biotechnology, for example, that already exist and can potentially be built on and exploited to encourage economic growth.

4 The term 'digital divide' may be attributable to Compaine (2001) and 'molecular divide' can be attributed to Louise Fresno, at the time Assistant Director-General at the FAO, in a speech in January 2003.

5 Science and technology exist to accumulate knowledge, layering facts in a more or less progressive way. This intellectual treadmill would not seem to sit well with scientists' claims of truth, or being sure, or of holding an assured viewpoint, when the accumulation of facts is in a state of almost constant flux. In this context, science and technology studies appropriate the engineering term of a 'black box', a predictable input-output device, something that requires no knowledge of the inner working of the device in order for it to be used. This idea will be explored in Chapter 2.

6 For example, Ferguson, 1990; Escobar, 1995; 1999; Rist, 1997.

Chapter 1

7 Amongst many sources, see Lall, 1996; Thompson and Thompson, 2000; Juma and Yee-Cheong, 2005.

8 See Ayala, 1995 for an overview of science in Latin America.

9 'Moore's law' is the best example of technological determinism. Moore (1965) described how the number of components on a microchip would double within a fixed period of time. This law then in some way fuelled the development of computers, and therefore information and communication technologies, and consequently impacted upon our lives.

10 See also Molony (2008a), who reaches similar conclusions regarding mobile phone use in Tanzania. Phones tend to be used for social networking and 'non-developmental' tasks.

11 There appears to be only one peer-reviewed paper that illustrates these yield increases. Non-peer reviewed Kenyan research indicates increases of 45 per cent.

12 Newer varieties of the hybrid maize matured earlier and, although this was a quality also desired by commercial farmers, it was the primary desire of subsistence farmers, as it allowed them to grow around dry periods more effectively.

Chapter 2

13 Remarks of Surgeon General Thomas Parran, 20 June 1946, cited in Staples, 2006: 134.

14 It is probably that the systematic spraying that took place elsewhere simply did not happen in Africa.

15 This was partly because this was the experience of US rice researchers in America.

16 See, for example, Anderson *et al.*, 1979; IRRI, 1979.

17 See, for example, Glaeser, 1987; Lipton and Longhurst, 1989; Conway, 1997. This is not in itself surprising, given the technical and yield-led focus of much of the Green Revolution research. Indeed, poorer farmers in developed countries also tend to take up new technologies less quickly and completely than richer farmers. See Buhler *et al.*, 2002.

18 Rejoice Mabudafhasi, South Africa's Deputy Minister of Environmental Affairs and Tourism, quoted in BBC News article, 'DDT and Africa's war on malaria', 26 November 2001.

19 Stephen Tohon, WHO Focal Point on Malaria in West Africa, quoted in IRIN press release, 'West Africa: new approach to malaria needed', 24 October 2007.

Chapter 3

20 See, for example, Chambers, 1979; Richards, 1985; Altieri, 1987.

21 See, for example, Shiva, 1993.

22 For example, Levi-Strauss, 1966 [1962].

23 It is, of course, easier to see relationships between 'scientific' and 'indigenous' in activities such as resource management than, say, healthcare, where

Shamanic interventions sit less well than modern ideas of medicine. Modern people still pray for the improved health of their relatives, though.

24 The 'Multiple Use System' work of IWMI, Khon Kaen University and local farmers' 'wisdom networks', collaborating to learn and develop new methods and technologies to manage water more effectively in northern Thailand, is a good example of the merging of 'technical' and 'indigenous' knowledge.

25 'Political ecology' can be traced back to the concern of peasant studies with the political economy of agrarian change, and the ground-breaking work of Michael Watts (1983) in uncovering the roots of famine in Nigeria, or possibly even earlier to the work of Claude Meillassoux on the impacts of colonialism on kinship (1981).

26 See for example, Adesina and Ouattara, 2000 for an overview of the multiple risks farmers have to manipulate and manage.

27 This sentence resonated strongly with 'actor-network theory' (ANT), a distinctive approach within science studies that tries to map relations that are simultaneously material and semiotic (most often interactions between technologies and people) and the networks they create. It has perhaps most successfully been used to explain how technologies 'come into being'. See for example, Latour, 1987, 1996.

28 See, for example, Freeman, 1987; Lundvall, 1992.

29 See, for example, Hall *et al.*, 2001; Clark, 2002.

30 For a discussion of the increasing role of NGOs in agricultural research, see Shrum, 2000.

31 Note that IDE also worked on introducing the treadle pump in India, where different organizational and institutional contexts, and a more rigid, managed approach, led to a rather different innovation experience.

32 A more complete description of the technology: 'The treadle pump is a foot-operated device that uses a flexible pipe (usually of bamboo or PVC) as a suction/tube well to pump water from shallow aquifers. It consists of a sheet metal or cast iron pump-head, a bamboo frame with two treadles and a bamboo or PVC strainer. The pump–head has two cylinders welded together with a single suction inlet at the bottom and two plungers with or without a rope and pulley. The cylinders are joined together at the base by a junction box, which connects through check valves to the suction pipe. As pedalling commences, water penetrates the filter and rises up through the suction pipe to the dynamic groundwater level. From there it is lifted in a pulsating stream following the strokes of the two pistons. The action of the two cylinders provides a virtually continuous stream of water. This makes it more efficient than single cylinder pumps. . . ' (Shah, 2000: 3).

33 See, for example, Horstkotte-Wesseler and Fischer (2000), who, in pointing to the risks of 'projectization', point to four key mitigants: (1) Creating systemic learning from project to project; (2) Creating a hierarchy of project priorities; (3) Avoiding replication of existing projects; and, (4) Embedding projects within local realities.

34 It is important to note that many rural regions, especially in sub-Saharan

Africa, remain poorly connected. Mobile phone use remains predominantly an urban activity.

35 Based on fieldwork conducted by Olga Morawczynski. See Mas and Morawczynski, 2009.

36 A Vodafone-sponsored study does link increasing mobile phone use to economic growth, but is not clear what the exact relationship between increasing mobile phone use and economic development actually is. See 'Africa: moving the debate forward' (Vodafone).

37 Again, methodology is an issue here. It is difficult to assess the relationship between increased ICT use and economic development (although clearly ICT has played roles in spheres like grassroots democracy and supporting other technological developments). See, for example, Avgerou, 2003.

38 'Market failure' is a pervasive but inaccurate term. The market not responding to market signals that simply do not register is not failure in any sense an economist would recognize.

39 This has not been the case for other global vaccine initiatives. In the past it has taken many decades for vaccines that have been administered in more developed countries to make it to less developed countries. Cf. Mursaskin, 1998.

40 For a clear exposition of the problems of development partnerships see Crewe and Harrison, 1998.

41 This is certainly borne out by the experience of the East Asian 'Tigers' like Korea and Taiwan, who developed strong indigenous firms in an array of sophisticated industries. Indeed, many rich countries used weak IPR protection in their early stages of industrialization to develop local technological bases, increasing protection as they approached the leaders

42 A different issue related to IPR is the 'mining' of indigenous knowledge for commercial gain. A good example of this is the case of the supposed appetite suppressant *Hoodia Gordoni* that had been used for thousands of years by the Bushmen of the Kalahari. The active ingredient was isolated and patented by a South African government agency that licensed the patent to two pharmaceutical companies. Only a public outcry resulted in Bushmen communities sharing in profits.

Chapter 4

43 'Food report criticises biofuel policies', *New York Times*, 30 May 2008.

44 'UN expert call biofuel "crime against humanity"', Associated Press, 27 October 2007.

45 Most forms of biofuels do demonstrate greenhouse gas savings over their life cycle compared to fossil fuels, with sugar cane ethanol, in particular, demonstrating large savings.

46 George Monbiot, *The Guardian*, 27 March 2007.

47 Lula da Silva, *The Guardian*, 31 May 2007.

48 Similarly to some of the examples cited in Chapter 2, the GM sweet potato promised spectacular yields and *ex ante* studies indicated more profits for farmers. In reality, the GM varieties of sweet potato performed less well than new traditionally bred varieties developed in Uganda (at considerably less cost).

49 The Kenyan framework also pre-dated the Cartagena Protocol on Biodiversity, ratified by Kenya in 2002, and a second phase of the UNEP project was tasked with addressing this issue, among others.

50 S. Singh, interview, 2005: 'Norman Borlaug: a billion lives saved'.

51 Quoted in *The Economist*, 'GM crops in Africa', 19 September 2002.

52 One of the reasons Malawi was so affected by the crisis was that the IMF and World Bank had urged it to sell its grain reserves to raise revenue for debt servicing.

53 The US–EU tension primarily revolves around regulatory differences between the two blocs. The EU developed its policy around the precautionary principle, which states that if an action might cause irreversible harm to society or the environment, in the absence of scientific consensus the burden of proof falls on those advocating or taking the action. The US position operates on the principle of 'substantial proof', as opposed to 'scientific consensus'. See Murphy and Levidow, 2006 for more detail.

54 See, for example, Gouse *et al.*, 2005; Marvier *et al.*, 2007.

55 It is interesting to note that the US refused to provide the funds for this milling. Zerbe (2004) argues that this is evidence that the US did indeed have an agenda to push the idea of GMO in these countries.

56 The make-up of civil society organizations consulted was relatively urban and middle-class.

57 Ann Veneman, USDA Statement, 30 August 2002.

58 Cited in Reuters Press Release, 20 January 2003.

59 'African farmers say GM crops are not the way forward', press release, 29 January 2006, IIED.

60 For a discussion see Richards, 2007.

61 For example, Escobar, 1995. See Yearley, 2005 for a critique of this critique of science.

Conclusion

62 According to MSF the impetus behind this decision was the embarrassment the drug companies would feel if the situation were to become public, something MSF had threatened to ensure. See for example, Juma and Yee-Cheong, 2005.

63 Sanafi-Aventis press release, 12 March 2007.

Bibliography

Abrahamsen, R. (2001) *Disciplining Democracy: Development Discourse and Good Governance in Africa*, Zed Books, London.

Abramovitz, M. (1989) *Thinking About Growth*, Cambridge University Press, Cambridge.

Action Aid (2003) 'GM crops – going against the grain', <www.actionaid.org>.

Adesina, A. and A. Ouattara (2000) 'Risk and agricultural systems in northern Côte d'Ivoire', *Agricultural Systems*, 66 (1): 17–32.

Agarwal, A. (1995). 'Dismantling the divide between indigenous and scientific knowledge', *Development and Change*, 26 (3): 413–29.

Aker, J. (2007) 'Does digital divide or provide? The impact of cell phones on grain markets in Niger', BREAD Working Paper, Center for International Development, Harvard University, Cambridge MA.

Allen, T. (2006) 'AIDS and evidence: interrogation of some Ugandan myths', *Journal of Biosocial Science*, 38 (1): 7–28.

Alston, J., S. Dehmer and P. Pardey (2006) 'International initiatives in agricultural R&D: the changing fortunes of the CGIAR' in P. Pardey, J. Aston and R. Piggot (eds), *Agricultural R&D in the Developing World: Too Little, Too Late?* IFPRI, Washington DC, pp. 313–60.

Altieri, M. (1987) *Agroecology: the Scientific Basis of Alternative Agriculture*, Westview Press, Boulder CO.

Anderson, R. (1991) 'The origins of the International Rice Research Institute', *Minerva*, 29 (1): 61–89.

Anderson, R., E. Levy and B. Morrison (1991) *Rice Science and Development Politics: Research Strategies and IRRI's Technologies Meet Asian Diversity*, Oxford University Press, Oxford.

Avgerou, C. (2003) 'The link between ICT and economic growth in the discourse of development' in M. Korpela, R. Montealegre and A. Poulymenakou (eds), *Organizational Information Systems in the Context of Globalization*, Kluwer Press, London, pp. 373–86.

Ayala, F. (1995) 'Science in Latin America', *Science*, 267 (5199): 826–7.

Bacchi, C., H. Natham, S. Hutner, P. McCann and A. Sjoerdsma (1980) 'Polyamine metabolism: a potential therapeutic target in trypanosomiasis', *Science*, 21: 332–4.

Barnes, B., D. Bloor and J. Henry (1996) *Scientific Knowledge: a Sociological Analysis*, Athlone Press, London.

Barnett, A. (2004) 'From "research" to poverty-reducing "innovation"', policy brief, Sussex Research Associates, Brighton.

Baum, W. (1986) *Partners Against Hunger: the Consultative Group on International Agriculture Research*, CGIAR, Washington DC.

Beck, U. (1992) *Risk Society: Towards a New Modernity*, Sage, London.

Berthoud, G. (1990) 'Modernity and development', *European Journal of Development Research*, 2: 22–35.

Bhabha, H. (1994) *The Location of Culture*, Routledge, London.

Blaikie, P. (1985) *Political Economy of Soil Erosion in Developing Countries*, Longman, London.

Blaikie, P., T. Cannon, T. Davis and B. Wisner (1994) *At Risk: Natural Hazards, People's Vulnerability, and Disasters*, Routledge, London.

Bloor, D. (1991) *Knowledge and Social Imagery*, University of Chicago Press, Chicago IL.

Brandt, W. (1980) *North–South: a Programme for Survival*, Pan, London.

Brown, G. (2004) 'Making globalisation work for all – the challenge of delivering the Monterrey consensus', speech delivered on 16 February, London.

Bryant, P. (2009) 'Deliberative governance: political fad or a vision of empowerment?' in C. Lyall, T. Papaioannou and J. Smith (eds), *The Limits to Governance: the Challenge of Policy-Making for the New Life Sciences*, Ashgate, London, pp. 239-60.

Buhler, W., S. Morse, E. Arthur, S. Bolton and J. Mann (2002) *Science, Agriculture and Research: a Compromised Participation?* Earthscan, London.

Buse, K. and G. Walt (2000) 'Global public–private partnerships: Part 1 – A new development in health?' *Bulletin of the World Health Organization*, 78 (4): 549–61.

Carson, R. (2002 [1962]) *Silent Spring*, Mariner Books, Boston.

Castells, M. (1998) *End of Millennium*, Volume 3. *The Information Age: Economy, Society and Culture*, Blackwell, London.

Cernea, M. (1988) 'Nongovernmental organizations and local development', World Bank Discussion Paper 40, World Bank, Washington DC.

Chambers, R. (1979) 'Rural development: whose knowledge counts?' *IDS Bulletin*, 10 (2).

—— (1980) 'Understanding professionals: small farmers and scientists', IADS Occasional Paper, International Agriculture Development Service, New York NY.

—— (1993) *Challenging the Professions: Frontiers for Rural Development*, Intermediate Technology Publications, London.

Chandler, R. (1992) *An Adventure in Applied Science: a History of the International Rice Research Institute*, IRRI, Los Baños.

Chataway, J. and J. Smith (2006) 'The International Aids Vaccine Initiative (IAVI): is it getting new science and technology to the world's neglected majority?' *World Development*, 34 (1): 16–30.

Chataway, J., J. Smith and D. Wield (2006) 'Science and technology partnerships and poverty alleviation in Africa', *International Journal of Technology Management and Sustainable Development*, 5 (2): 103–23.

Chataway, J., D. Kale and D. Wield (2007a) 'The Indian pharmaceutical industry before and after TRIPS', *Technology Analysis and Strategic Management*, 19 (5): 559–63.

Chataway, J., J. Smith and D. Wield (2007b) 'Shaping scientific excellence in agricultural research', *International Journal of Biotechnology*, 9 (2), 172–87.

Clark, N. (2002) 'Innovation systems, technology assessment and the new knowledge market: implications for Third World development', *Journal of the Economics of Innovation and New Technology*, 11 (4/5): 353–68

Clark, N., G. Naik and A. Hall (2002) 'The establishment of treadle pumps in Bangladesh and India: a comparative study', paper presented at the Annual Meeting of the UK Development Studies Association, September 2003.

Clark, N., A. Hall, R. Sulamain and G. Naik (2003) 'Research as capacity building: the case of an NGO facilitated post-harvest innovation system for the Himalayan hills', *World Development*, 31 (11): 1845–63.

Clark, N., J. Mugabe and J. Smith (2007a) *Biotechnology Policy in Africa*, ACTS Press, Nairobi.

Clark, N., J. Smith and M. Hirvonen (2007b) 'Livestock R&D in East and Southern Africa: an innovation systems perspective with special reference to ILRI', *International Journal of Technology Management and Sustainable Development*, 6 (1): 9–23.

Cleaver, H. (1972) 'The contradictions of the Green Revolution', *The American Economic Review*, 72: 177–88.

Collins, H. and R. Evans (2002) 'The third wave of science studies: studies of expertise and experience', *Social Studies of Science*, 32 (2): 235–96.

Commission for Africa (2005) *Our Common Interest. Report of the Commission for Africa*, Penguin, London.

Compaine, B. (2001) *The Digital Divide: Facing a Crisis or Creating a Myth?* MIT Press, Cambridge MA.

Conway, G. (1987) *The Doubly Green Revolution*, Penguin, London.

Cottan, C. and E. Higgins (1946) 'DDT and its effect on fish and wildlife', *Journal of Economic Etymology*, 39: 44–52.

Coyne, P. (2001) 'The eflornithine story', *Journal of the American Academy of Dermatology*, 45: 784–6.

Crewe, E. and E. Harrison (1998) *Whose Development? An Ethnography of Aid*, Zed Books, London.

Cullather, N. (2004) 'Miracles of modernization: the Green Revolution and the apotheosis of technology', *Diplomatic History*, 28 (2): 227–54.

De Almeida, E., J. Bomtempo and C. De Souza de Silva (2007) 'The performance of Brazilian biofuels: an economic, environmental and social analysis', Discussion Paper No. 2007–5, Organization for Economic Cooperation and Development (OECD).

DFID (2005) 'To know what to do: DFID research funding framework, 2005–2007', Department for International Development, London.

Diederen, P., H. van Meijl, A. Wolters and K. Bijak (2003) 'Innovation adoption in agriculture: innovators, early adopters and laggards', *Cahiers d'économie et sociologie rurales*, 67: 30–50.

DiMasi, J., R. Hansen and H. Grabowski (2003) 'The price of innovation: new estimates of drug development costs', *Journal of Health Economics*, 22: 151–85.

Donner, J. (2007) 'Customer acquisition among small and informal businesses in urban India: comparing face to face and mediated channels', *Electronic Journal of Information Systems in Developing Countries*, 32 (3): 1–16.

Edelman, M. and A. Haugerud (2005) 'Introduction: the anthropology of development and globalisation' in M. Edelman and A. Haugerud (eds), *The Anthropology of Development and Globalisation: from Classical Political Economy to Contemporary Neoliberalism*, Blackwell Publishing, London, pp. 1–74.

Eicher, C. (1995) 'Zimbabwe's maize-based Green Revolution: preconditions for replication', *World Development*, 23 (5): 805–18.

Erikkson Baaz, M. (2005) *The Paternalism of Partnership: a Postcolonial Reading of Identity in Development Aid*, Zed Books, London.

Escobar, A. (1995) *Encountering Development. the Making and Unmaking of the Third World*, Princeton University Press, Princeton NJ.

—— (1999) 'After nature: steps to an anti-essentialist political ecology', *Current Anthropology*, 40 (1): 1–30.

Esteva, G. (1996) 'Hosting the otherness of the other: the case of the Green Revolution' in F. Appfel-Marglin and S. Marglin (eds), *Decolonizing Knowledge: from Development to Dialogue*, Oxford University Press, Oxford, pp. 249–78.

Evenson, R. and D. Gollin (2003) 'Assessing the impact of the Green Revolution, 1960 to 2000', *Science*, 300 (May): 758–62.

Ferguson, J. (1990) *The Anti-Politics Machine: 'Development', Depoliticization and Bureaucratic Power in Lesotho*, Cambridge University Press, Cambridge.

—— (1999) *Expectations of Modernity: Myths and Meanings of Urban Life in the Zambian Copperbelt*, University of California Press, Los Angeles CA.

—— (2004) *Empire: How Britain Made the Modern World*, Penguin, London.

—— (2006) *Global Shadows: Africa in the Neoliberal World Order*, Duke University Press, Durham NC.

Fitzgerald, D. (1996) 'Exporting American agriculture: the Rockefeller Foundation in Mexico, 1943–1953', *Social Studies of Science*, 16 (4): 457–83.

Forbes, N. and D. Wield (2002) *From Followers to Leaders: Managing Technology and Innovation*, Routledge, London.

Foucault, M. (1979) *Discipline and Punish*, Vintage, New York NY.

Fowler, A. (2000) 'Civil society, NGDOs and social development', Occasional Paper 1, United Nations Research Institute for Social Development (UNRISD), Geneva.

Freeman, C. (1987) *Technology and Economic Performance: Lessons from Japan*, Pinter Publishers, London.

Freeman, H., F. Ellis and E. Allison (2004) 'Livelihoods and rural poverty reduction in Kenya', *Development Policy Review,* 22 (2): 147–71.

GFHR (1999) 'The 10/90 Report on Health Research, 1999', Global Forum for Health Research, Geneva.

Gibbons, M., C. Limoges, H. Nowotny, S. Schwartzman, P. Scott and M. Trow (1994) *The New Production of Knowledge: the Dynamics of Science and Research in Contemporary Societies,* Sage Publications, London.

Giddens, A. (2002) *Runaway World,* Profile Books, London.

Glaeser, B. (1987) *The Green Revolution Revisited: Critiques and Alternatives,* Allen and Unwin, London.

Gouse, M., C. Pray, J. Kirsten and D. Schimmelpfennig (2005) 'A GM subsistence crop in Africa: the case of Bt white maize in South Africa', *International Journal of Biotechnology,* 7 (1–3): 84–94.

GRAIN (2007) 'The new scramble for Africa', GRAIN, July.

Hall, A. (2007) 'Challenges to strengthening agricultural innovation systems: where do we go from here?', paper presented at the 'Farmer First Revisited' workshop, held at the University of Sussex, 12–14 December.

Hall, A., G. Brockett, S. Tayor, M. Sivamohan and N. Clark (2001) 'Why research partnerships really matter: innovation theory, institutional arrangements and implications for developing new technology for the poor', *World Development,* 29 (5): 783–97.

Harrar, J. (1958) 'International Rice Research Centre', Royal Agricultural College archive, 5 October.

Harrar, J., P. Mangelsdorf and W. Weaver (1952) 'Notes on Indian Agriculture', Royal Agricultural College archive, 11 April, pp. 25-6.

Harsh, M. (2005) 'Formal and informal governance of agricultural biotechnology in Kenya: participation and accountability in controversy surrounding the draft biosafety bill', *Journal of International Development,* 17 (5): 661–77.

Hirvonen, M. (2005) 'Institutional responses to an emerging mode 2 context in international agricultural research: the case of ILRI', UNU Merit/Innogen, Edinburgh.

Horstkotte-Wesseler, G. and D. Byerlee (2000) 'Agricultural biotechnology and the poor: the role of development assistance agencies' in M. Qaim, A. Krattiger and J. von Braun (eds) *Agricultural Biotechnology in Developing Countries: Towards Optimizing the Benefits for the Poor,* Kluwer Academic Publishers, Dordrecht.

House of Commons (2004) *The Use of Science in UK International Development Policy. Volumes 1 and 2.* Science and Technology Committee, House of Commons, London.

ILRAD (1992) 'ILRAD 1991: Annual Report of the International Laboratory for Research on Animal Diseases'. International Laboratory for Research on Animal Diseases, Nairobi.

IRRI (1962) 'Annual Report. 1961–1962', International Rice Research Institute, Los Baños.

—— (1966) 'Annual Report. 1965–1966', International Rice Research Institute, Los Baños.

—— (1979) 'Research Highlights', International Rice Research Institute, Los Baños.

IRRI (1985) 'International Rice Research: 25 Years of Highlights,' International Rice Research Institute, Los Baños.
—— (1992) 'Sharing Responsibilities, 1991–1992', International Rice Research Institute, Los Baños.
Jasanoff, S. (1999) 'The songlines of risk', *Environmental Values*, 8 (2): 135–52.
Jensen, R. (2007) 'The digital provide: information (technology), market performance and welfare in the south Indian fisheries sector', *Quarterly Journal of Economics*, 122 (3), 879–924.
Jessop, B. (1998) 'The rise of governance and the risks of failure: the case of economic development', *International Social Sciences Journal*, 50 (155): 30–45.
Jordan, A., R. Wurzel and A. Zito (2005) 'The rise of "new" policy instruments in comparative perspective: has governance eclipsed government?' *Political Studies*, 53 (3): 477–96.
Juma, C. and N. Clark (2002) 'Technological catch-up: opportunities and challenges for developing countries', SUPRA Working Paper 28, Edinburgh.
Juma, C. and L. Yee-Cheong (2005) *Innovation: Applying Knowledge in Development, Taskforce 10*, Earthscan, London.
Knorr-Cetina, K. (1981) *The Manufacture of Knowledge: an Essay on the Constructivist and Contextual Nature of Science*, Pergamon Press, Oxford.
Kothari, U. (2005) 'Authority and expertise: the professionalisation of international development and the ordering of dissent', *Antipode*, 37 (3): 425–46.
Kremer, M. and R. Glennerster (2004) *Strong Medicine: Creating Incentives for Pharmaceutical Research on Neglected Diseases*, Princeton University Press, Princeton NJ.
Lall, S. (1996) *Learning from the Asian Tigers: Studies in Technology and Industrial Policy*, Palgrave Macmillan, London.
—— (2001) 'Indicators of the relative importance of IPRs in developing countries', UNCTAD/ICTSD Capacity Building Project on 'Intellectual Property Rights and Sustainable Development'.
Latour, B. (1987) *Science in Action: How to Follow Scientists and Engineers through Society*, Harvard University Press, Cambridge MA.
—— (1992) 'Where are the missing masses? The sociology of a few mundane artefacts' in W. Bijker and J. Laws (eds), *Shaping Technology/Building Society: Studies in Sociotechnical Change*, MIT Press, Cambridge MA and London, pp. 225–58
—— (1996) *Aramis: Or the Love of Technology?* Harvard University Press, Cambridge MA.
Leach, M. (2007) 'Science and politics: accommodating dissent', *Nature*, 450 (7169): 483–4.
Leach, M. and I. Scoones (2006) *The Slow Race: Making Technology Work for the Poor*, Demos, London.
Leach, M., I. Scoones and B. Wynne (2005) 'Introduction: science, citizenship and globalization' in M. Leach, I. Scoones and B. Wynne (eds),

Science and Citizens: Globalization and the Challenge of Engagement, Zed Books, London, pp. 3–14.

Lévi-Strauss, C. (1966 [1962]) *The Savage Mind,* University of Chicago Press, Chicago IL.

Lipton, M. and R. Longhurst (1989) *New Seeds and Poor People,* Unwin Hyman, London.

Lundvall, B. (1992) *National Systems of Innovation and Interactive Learning,* Pinter Publishers, London.

Lyall, C. and J. Tait (2005) *New Modes of Governance: Developing an Integrated Policy Approach to Science, Technology, Risk and the Environment,* Ashgate, Aldershot.

Maguire, S. (2004) 'The co-evolution of technology and discourse: a study of substitution processes for the insecticide DDT', *Organization Studies,* 25 (1): 113–34.

Makinda, S. (2007) 'How Africa can benefit from knowledge', *Futures,* 39 (8): 973–85.

Manyong, V., A. Alene, A. Olanrewaju, B. Ayedun, V. Rweyendela, A. Wesonga, G. Omanya, H. Mignouna and M. Bokanga (2007) 'Study of *striga* control using IR maize in Western Kenya', AATF/IITA *Striga Control Project,* Nairobi.

Marglin, S. (1996) 'Farmers, seedsmen and scientists: systems of agriculture and systems of knowledge' in F. Appfel-Marglin and S. Marglin (eds), *Decolonizing Knowledge: from Development to Dialogue,* Oxford University Press, Oxford, pp. 185–248.

Marvier, M., C. McCreedy, J. Regetz and P. Kareiva (2007) 'A meta-analysis of effects of Bt cotton and maize on nontarget invertebrates', *Science,* 316/5830: 1475–7.

Mas, I. and O. Morawczynski (2009) 'Designing mobile money services: lessons from M-PESA', *Innovations: Technology, Governance, Globalization,* 4 (2): 77-91.

Mashingaidze, K. (1994) 'Maize research and development' in R. Mandivamba and C. Eicher (eds) *Zimbabwe's Agricultural Revolution,* University of Zimbabwe Publications, Harare.

Maskus, K. (2000) 'Intellectual property rights in the global economy', Institute for International Economics, Washington DC.

Mazrui, A. and A. White (1988) 'Gender, skill and power: Africa in search of transformation' in A. Adedeji, O. Teriba and P. Bugembe (eds), *The Challenge of African Economic Recovery and Development,* Frank Cass, London, pp. 353–73.

McCann, J. (2005) *Maize and Grace: Africa's Encounter with a New World Crop, 1500–2000,* Harvard University Press, Cambridge MA.

McNamara, K. (2003) 'Information and communication technologies, knowledge and development: learning from experience', background paper for InfoDev Annual Symposium, 9–10 December, Geneva.

Meier, R. (2000) 'Late-blooming societies can be stimulated by information technologies', *Futures,* 32: 163–81.

Meillassoux, C. (1981) *Maidens, Meal and Money: Capitalism and the Domestic Community,* Cambridge University Press, Cambridge.

Mercer, C. (2005) 'Telecentres and transformations: modernizing Tanzania through the Internet', *African Affairs*, 105/419: 243–64.

Miller, D. and D. Slater (2001) *The Internet: an Ethnographic Approach*, Berg, London.

Mitchell, D. (2008) 'A note on rising food prices, prepared for the World Bank, 8 April 2008' [leaked draft report].

Molony, T. (2008a) 'Non-development uses of mobile communication in Tanzania', in J. Katz (ed.), *The Handbook of Mobile Communication Studies*, MIT Press, Cambridge MA, pp. 339–52.

—— (2008b) 'Running out of credit: the limitations of mobile telephony in a Tanzanian agricultural marketing system', *Journal of Modern African Studies*, 46 (4): 637–58.

Moore, G. (1965) 'Cramming more components onto integrated circuits', *Electronics*, 38: 114–17.

Mosse, D. (2004) *Cultivating Development: an Ethnography of Aid Policy and Practice*, Zed Books, London.

Mugabe, J. (2003) 'Centers of excellence in science and technology for Africa's sustainable development', NEPAD Science and Technology Secretariat, Pretoria.

Muraskin, W. (1998) *The Politics of International Health: the Children's Vaccine Initiative and the Struggle to Develop Vaccines for the Third World*, SUNY Press, New York NY.

Murphy, J. and L. Levidow (2006) *Governing the Transatlantic Conflict over Agricultural Biotechnology: Contending Coalitions, Trade Liberalisation and Standard Setting*, Routledge, London.

Nelson, R. and S. Winter (1982) *An Evolutionary Theory of Economic Change*, Harvard University Press, Cambridge MA.

New Scientist (2004) 'Feeding Africa', 27 May 2000.

Nightingale, A. (2005) '"The experts taught us all we know": professionalisation and knowledge in Nepalese community forestry', *Antipode*, 37 (3): 581–604.

Niosi, J. and S. Reid (2007) 'Biotechnology and nanotechnology: science-based enabling technologies as windows of opportunity for LDCs?' *World Development*, 35 (3): 426–38.

Odame, H., P. Kameri-Mbote, and D. Wafula (2003) 'Innovation and policy process: the case of transgenic sweet potato in Kenya', African Centre of Technology Studies, Nairobi.

Orsenigo, L., G. Pisano and R. Henderson (1999) 'The pharmaceutical industry and the revolution in molecular biology: exploring the interactions between scientific, institutional and organizational change' in D. Mowery and R. Nelson (eds), *The Sources of Industrial Advantages*, Cambridge University Press, Cambridge.

Oxfam (2002) 'Rigged rules and double standards: trade, globalisation, and the fight against poverty', Oxfam, Oxford.

—— (2008) 'Another inconvenient truth: how biofuel policies are deepening poverty and accelerating climate change', Oxfam Briefing Paper 114, Oxford.

Pardey, P., S. Dehmer and S. Feki (2006) 'Global spending on science: A new order in the making?' International Science and Technology Practice and Policy (InSTePP) Center, University of Minnesota, St Paul.

Pepin, J., F. Milford, C. Guern and P. Schechter (1987) 'Difluoro-methylornithine for arseno-resistant *Trypanosoma brucei gambiense* sleeping sickness', *Lancet*, 2: 1431–3.

Perkins, J. (1997) *Geopolitics and the Green Revolution: Wheat, Genes and the Cold War,* Oxford University Press, New York NY.

Peters, P. (2002) 'The limits of knowledge: securing rural livelihoods in a situation of resource scarcity' in C. Barrett, F. Place and A. Aboud (eds), *Natural Resource Management Practices in African Agriculture: Understanding and Improving Current Practices,* CABI Publishing, Cambridge.

Pierre, J. and B. Peters (2000) *Governance, Politics and the State,* Macmillan Press, London.

Public Papers of the Presidents of the United States (1964) *Harry S. Truman, Year 1949,* 5, United States Government Printing Office, Washington DC.

Qaim, M. (1999) 'Assessing the impact of banana biotechnology in Kenya'. Brief No. 10, ISAAA, New York NY.

Redner, H. (1994) *A New Science of Representation: Towards an Integrated Theory of Representation in Science, Politics and Art,* Westview, Boulder CO.

Richards, P. (1985) *Indigenous Agricultural Revolution,* Methuen, London.

—— (1989) 'Agriculture as performance' in R. Chambers, A. Pacey and L. A. Thrupp (eds), *Farmer First: Farmer Innovation and Agricultural Research,* Intermediate Technology Publications, London, pp. 39–51.

—— (2007) 'How does participation work? Deliberation and performance in African food security', *IDS Bulletin,* 38 (5): 21–35.

Rist, G. (1997) *The History of Development: from Western Origins to Global Faith,* Zed Books, London.

Rohwer, S. (1945) 'Report of the special committee on DDT with S. A. Rowher as chairman', *Journal of Economic Entomology,* 38: 144.

Rosaldo, R. (1995) 'Foreword', in G. Canclini (ed.), *Hybrid Cultures: Strategies for Entering and Leaving Modernity,* University of Minneapolis Press, Minneapolis MN.

Rosenberg, T. (2006) 'The scandal of "poor people's diseases"', *New York Times,* 29 March 2006.

Rostow, W. W. (1960) *The Stages of Economic Growth: a Non-Communist Manifesto,* Cambridge University Press, Cambridge.

Russell, R. (1952) *Malaria: Basic Principles Briefly Stated,* Blackwell, Oxford.

Ruttan, V. (1977) 'The Green Revolution: seven generalizations', *International Development Review,* 19: 16–23.

Schumacher, E. F. (1973) *Small is Beautiful: Economics As If People Mattered,* Hartley and Marks, London.

Scudder, K. (2005) *The Future of Large Dams: Dealing with Social, Environmental, Institutional and Political Costs,* Earthscan, London.

Shah, T. (2000) 'Pedal pump and the poor: social impact of a manual irrigation technology in South Asia', International Development Enterprises (IDE), New Delhi.

Shiva, V. (1991a) 'The green revolution in the Punjab', *The Ecologist*, 21(March/April): 57–60.

—— (1991b) *The Violence of the Green Revolution: Third World Agriculture, Ecology and Politics*, Zed Books, London.

—— (1993) *Monocultures of the Mind: Perspectives on Biodiversity and Biotechnology*, Zed Books, London.

Shrum, W. (2000) 'Science and story in development: the emergence of non-governmental organisations in agricultural research', *Social Studies of Science*, 30 (1): 95–124.

Simonetti, R., E. Archambault, C. Grégoire, and D. Kale (2007) 'The dynamics of pharmaceutical patenting in India: evidence from USPTO data', *Technology Analysis and Strategic Management*, 19 (5): 625–42.

Sismondo, S. (2004) *An Introduction to Science and Technology Studies*, Blackwell, Oxford.

Smith, J. (2003) 'Povertà, potere e resistenza: sicurezza alimentare e sovranità in Africa Australe', *Afriche e Orienti*, 2: 158–72.

—— (2005) 'Context-bound knowledge production, capacity building and new product networks', *Journal of International Development*, 17 (5): 647–59.

—— (2007) 'Culturing development: bananas, petri dishes and "mad science"', *Journal of Eastern African Studies*, 1 (2): 212–33.

Smith, M. and L. Marx (1994) *Does Technology Drive History? The Dilemma of Technological Determinism*, MIT Press, Cambridge MA.

Snapp, S., G. Kanyama-Phiri, B. Kamanga, R. Gilbert and K. Wellard (2002) 'Farmer and researcher partnerships in Malawi: developing soil fertility technologies for the near-term and far-term', *Experimental Agriculture*, 38: 411–31.

Sorj, B. (1991) 'Modernity and social disintegration: crisis of society and crisis of the social sciences in Brazil and Latin America', *European Journal of Development Research*, 21: 108–20.

Staples, A. (2006) *The Birth of Development: How the World Bank, Food and Agriculture Organization, and World Health Organization Changed the World, 1945–1965*, Kent State University Press, Kent OH.

Stiglitz, J. (2002) *Making Globalization Work*, W. W. Norton, New York NY.

Stoker, G. (1998) 'Governance as theory: five propositions', *International Social Science Journal*, 50: 17–28.

Thompson, N. and S. Thompson (2000) *The Baobab and the Mango Tree: Lessons About Development – African and Asian Contrasts*, Zed Books, London.

Torr, S., J. Hargrove and G. Vale (2005) 'Towards a rational policy for dealing with Tsetse', *Trends in Parasitology*, 11: 537–41.

United Nations Development Programme (UNDP) (2001) *Human Development Report: Making New Technologies Work for Development*, Oxford University Press, New York NY.

Vaughan, M. (1991) *Curing Their Ills: Colonial Power and African Illness*, Polity Press, Cambridge.

Vidal, J. (2002) 'US dumping "unsold GM food on Africa"', *The Guardian*, 7 October.

Vogel, C. and J. Smith (2002) 'The politics of scarcity: conceptualising the current food security crisis in southern Africa', *South African Journal of Science*, 98 (7/8): 315–17.

Wade, N. (1974) 'Green Revolution (I): a just technology, often unjust in use', *Science*, 186: 1093–6.

Wagner, C., I. Brahmakulam, B. Jackson, A. Wong and T. Yoda (2001) 'Science and technology collaboration: building capacity in developing countries?', RAND, Santa Monica.

Wakeford, T. and M. Pimbert (2004) 'Prajateerpu, power and knowledge: the politics of participatory action research in development', *Action Research*, 2 (1): 25–46.

Wambugu, F. (2001) *Modifying Africa: How Biotechnology Can Benefit the Poor and Hungry – a Case Study from Kenya*, Imprelibros, Nairobi.

Wambugu, F. and R. Kiome (2001) 'The benefits of biotechnology for small-scale producers in Kenya', Brief No. 22, International Service for the Acquisition of Agri-Biotech Applications, New York NY.

Watts, M. (1983) *Silent Violence: Food, Famine and the Peasantry in Northern Nigeria*, University of California Press, Berkeley CA.

—— (2001) '1968 and all that...', *Progress in Human Geography*, 25 (2): 157–88.

Wetlands International (2006) 'Bio-fuels less sustainable than realised', press release for report, 'Assessment of CO_2 emissions from drained peatlands in SE Asia'.

Winrock (1992) 'Assessment of Animal Agriculture in sub-Saharan Africa', Winrock International Institute for Agricultural Development, Arkansas.

World Bank (1994) 'Governance: the World Bank's experience', World Bank, Washington DC.

—— (1999) *Knowledge for Development: World Development Report 1998/99*, Oxford University Press, New York NY.

—— (2001) 'Intellectual property: balancing incentives with competitive access', *Global Economic Prospects*: 129–50.

—— (2008) 'Rising food prices: policy options and the World Bank response', background note, April 2008, World Bank, Washington DC.

World Health Organization (2000) 'Health systems: improving performance' in 'World Health Report 2000', World Health Organization, Geneva.

—— (2007) 'Working for health: an introduction to the World Health Organization', United Nations, Geneva.

Wynne, B. (1992) 'Uncertainty and environmental learning', *Global Environmental Change*, 2: 111–27.

Yayha, M. (2007) 'Polio vaccines – "no thank you!": barriers to polio eradication in Northern Nigera', *African Affairs*, 106 (423): 185–204.

Yearley, S. (2005) *Making Sense of Science: Understanding the Social Study of Science*, Sage, London.

Zerbe, N. (2004) 'Feeding the famine? American food aid and the GMO debate in Southern Africa', *Food Policy*, 29: 593–608.

Zoellnick, R. (2003) 'United States v. European Union', *The Wall Street Journal*, 21 May 2003.

Index

www.ingramcontent.com/pod-product-compliance
Lightning Source LLC
Chambersburg PA
CBHW070345270326
41926CB00017B/3990